Introductions

These paintings are specially made for a Christmas edition in the michael Andrew Law's pale hair girls series ,these are one of the few comic-fine art crossover works by michael Andrew law.

Law chosen half innocent ,half erotic manga or comic's young female figures interacted with famous cities and landmarks which symbolizes the color and the materials heavy of contemporary Christmas holidays .

Pale hair girls are the most ambitious project to date by michael Andrew law, which begins with 60 oil paintings for the acclaimed iegoism one man show, which later spawned into a 900 plus more digital-classical crossover paintings , most of the earliest in this series are done solely in oil and sometimes with acrylic based underpainting ,while later works uses more variety of materials such as glitter , gold leafs, die cuts ,sometimes museum quality achieve prints to interact with the oil and acrylic paint.

At the time when Law started working on these paintings ,he was just fresh out of his art school practice of classical oil painting in the mid 2000s in Hong Kong that's when he still using some of the academic classical painting method which he extensively trained during his art school years.that explains why These earliest work in the pale hair girls series were and mostly uses live model sitters in studio , which later on as the series expands,the later works are mostly painted based on photographs.

In the series , Law also took some of the portraits painted works from his school years, and turned them into the same visual interpretation and style with the series , a gestures,in his words ,to erases the identities of the portraits , and in attempt to creating a timelessness vibe which cooperate with the pale hair girl's identitylessness of this series.

While Michael Andrew Law obsessed with classical aesthetic figures , he also tries to pay homage to modern art superstars such as Warhol , litchenstein, richter , de Kooning, utilizing a more contemporary visual styles of images to document and expressed the contemporary predicament of his own generation - the post handover of the 2000s of Hong Kong - also cited as the most polarizing era of Hong Kong in many different subjects such as differences of political views, differences in contemporary economics situation between generations , cultural disagreement between generations and cultural differences between countries, resulting feeling and realistically of unfairness , arguments ,disappointments and finger pointing in between all of above and more.

Images in this Christmas edition picture book are also available as posters , limited edition prints ,if you interested in purchasing works or limited edition published in this book , please simply send email to info@michaelandrewlaw.com , and simply tell us this volume's book name and the plate number , we will inform you regarding the picture 's availability as soon as possible.Other merchandise such as T-shirts , DVDs, stickers , calendar and other michael Andrew Law collectable items, please go to michaelandrewlaw.com or Google keywords "Michael Andrew Law" for further information.

PLATE No.

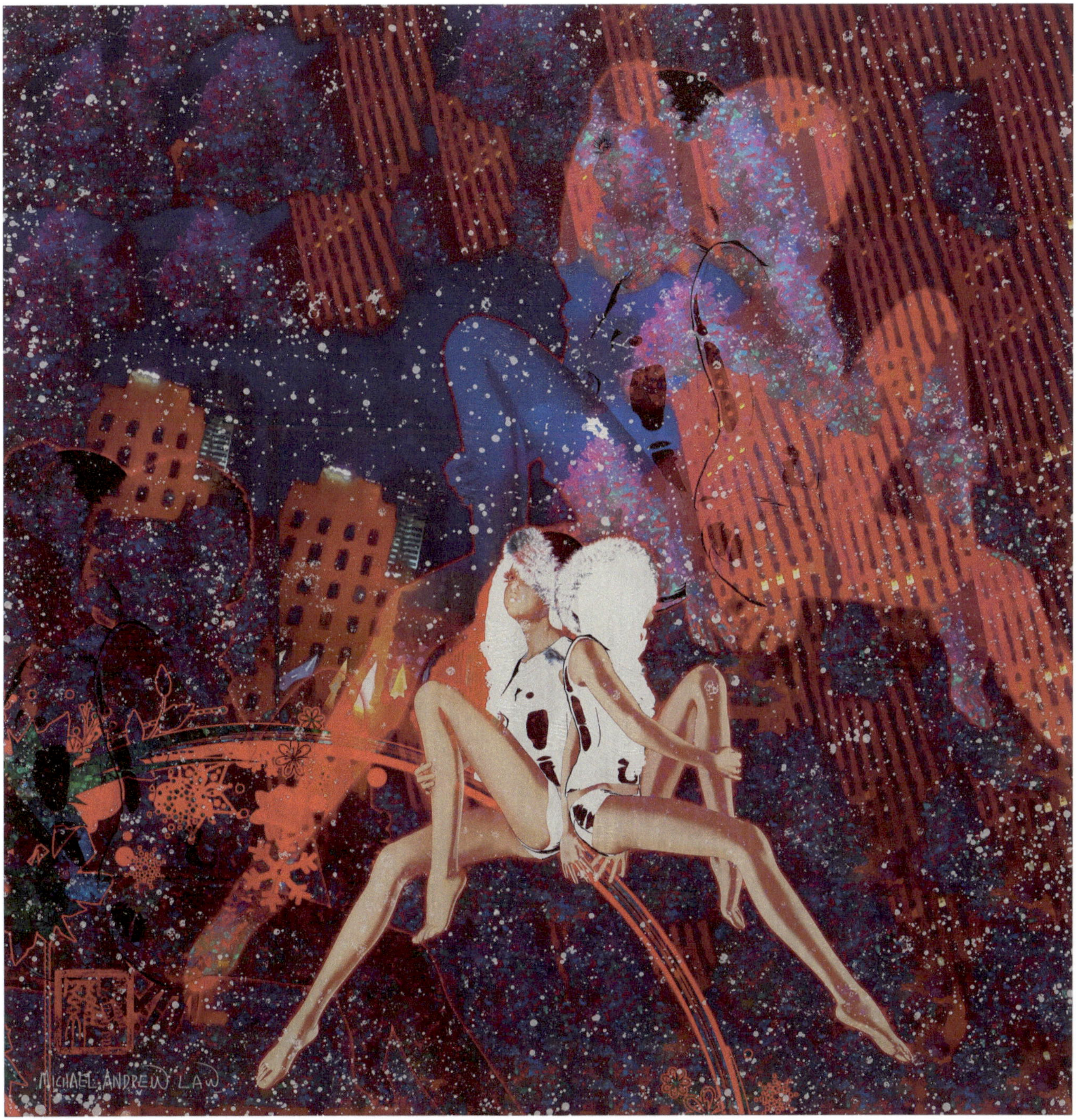

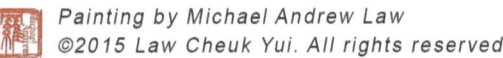

am I allowed to go Christmas shopping?

PLATE No.

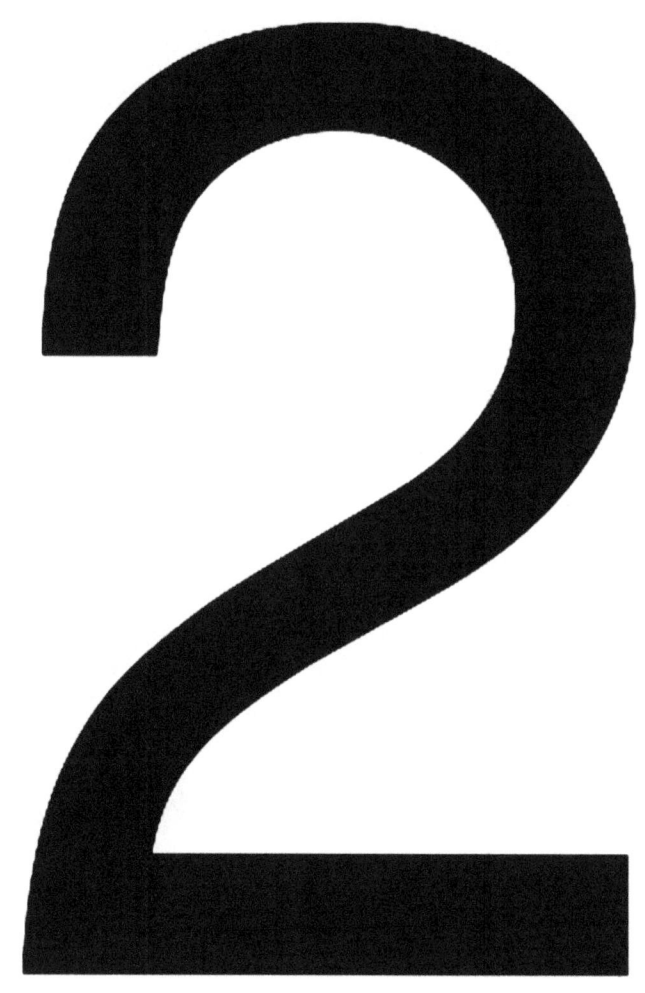

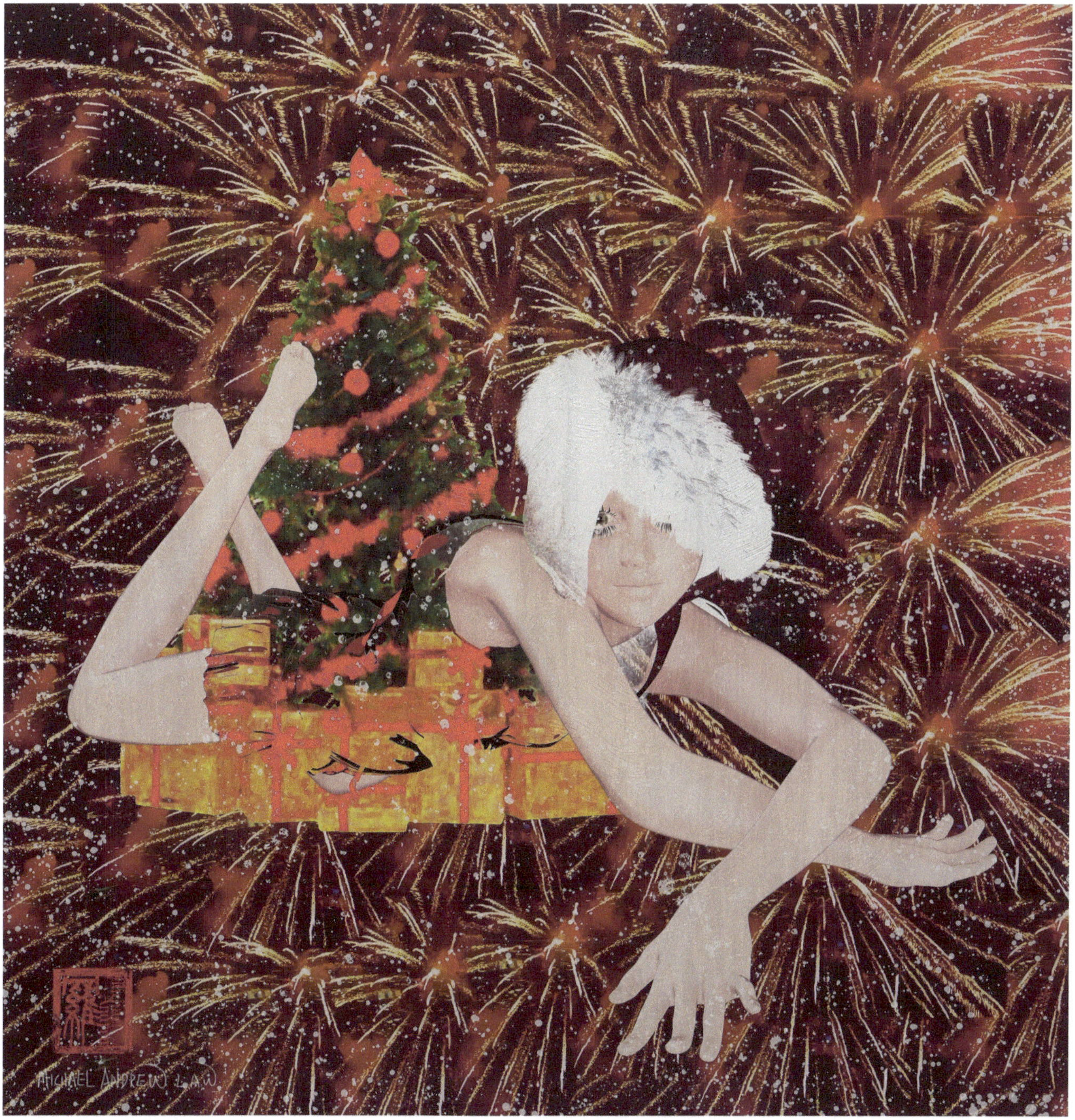

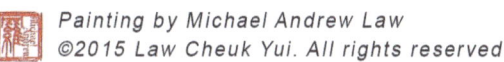

I have always thought of Christmas time

Painting by Michael Andrew Law
©2015 Law Cheuk Yui. All rights reserved

PLATE No.

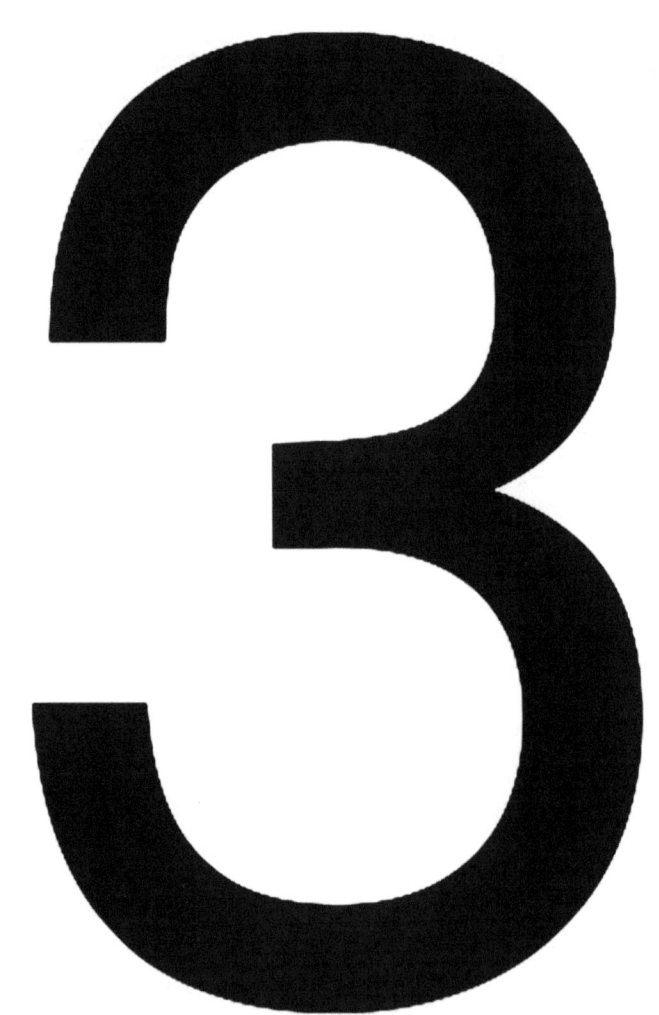

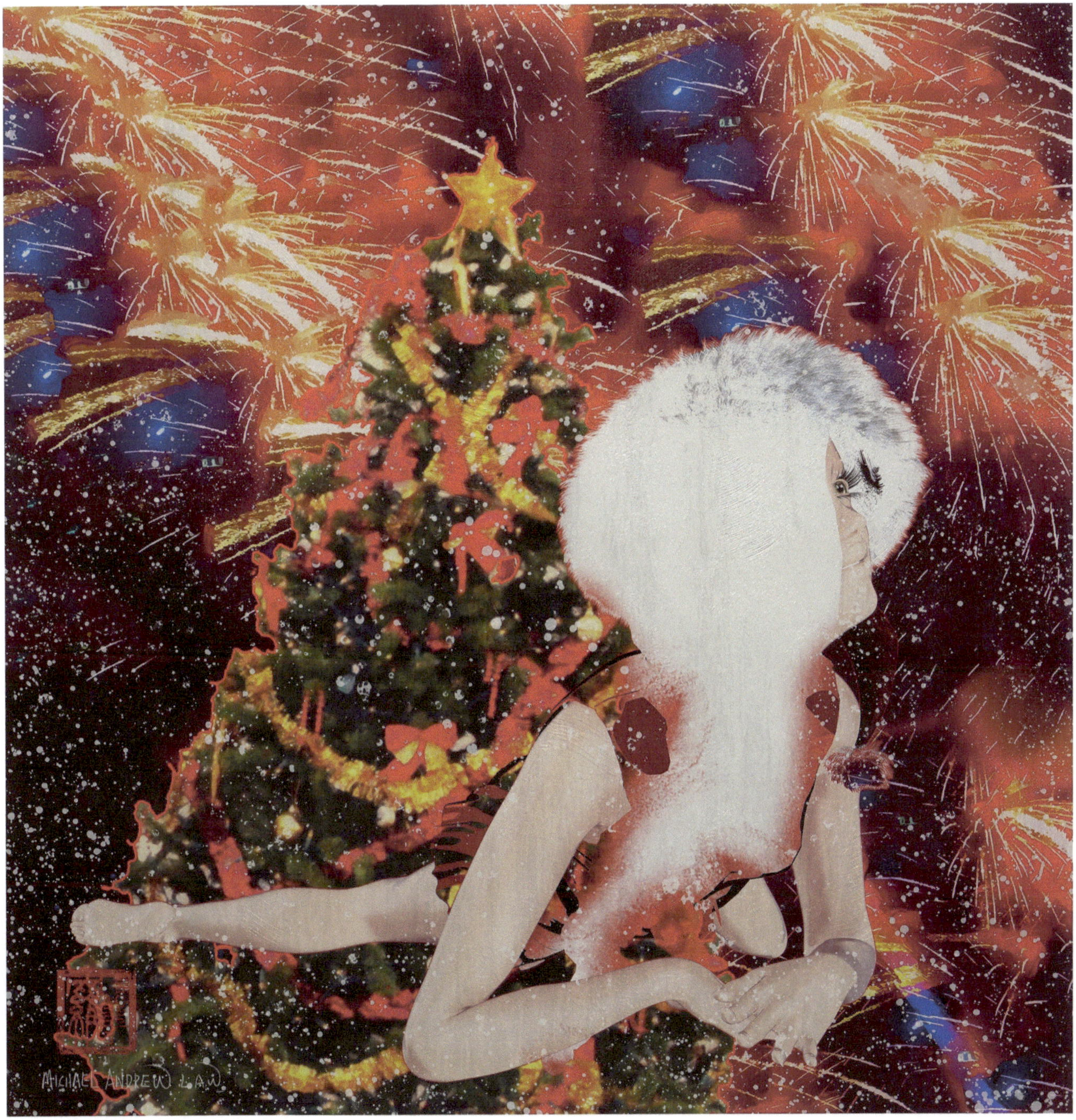

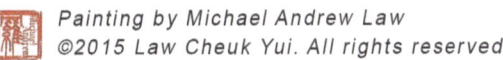

It is Christmas in the heart that puts Christmas in the air.

Painting by Michael Andrew Law

PLATE No.

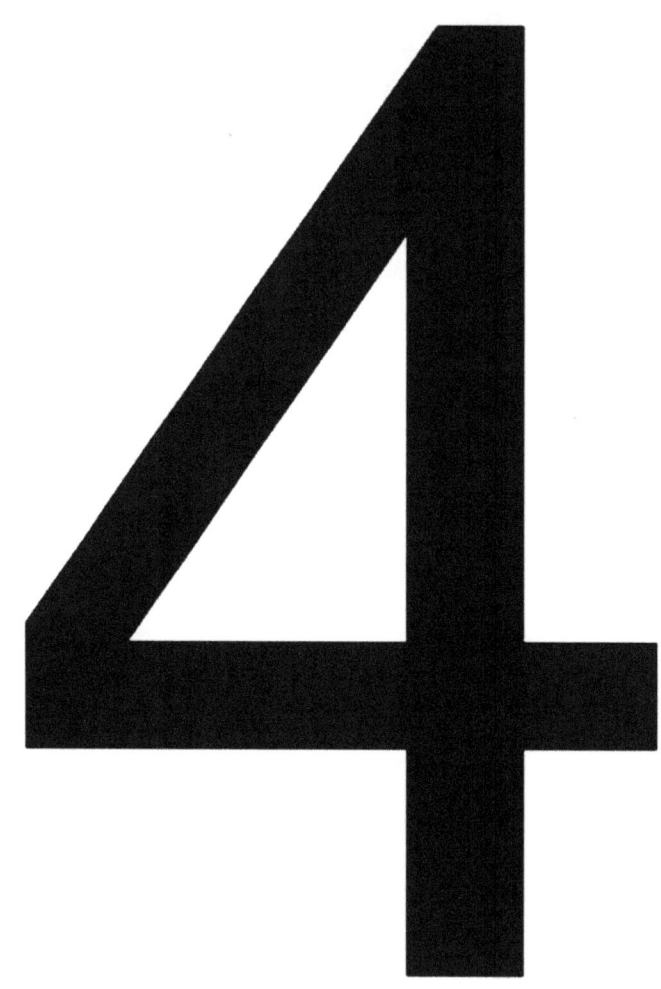

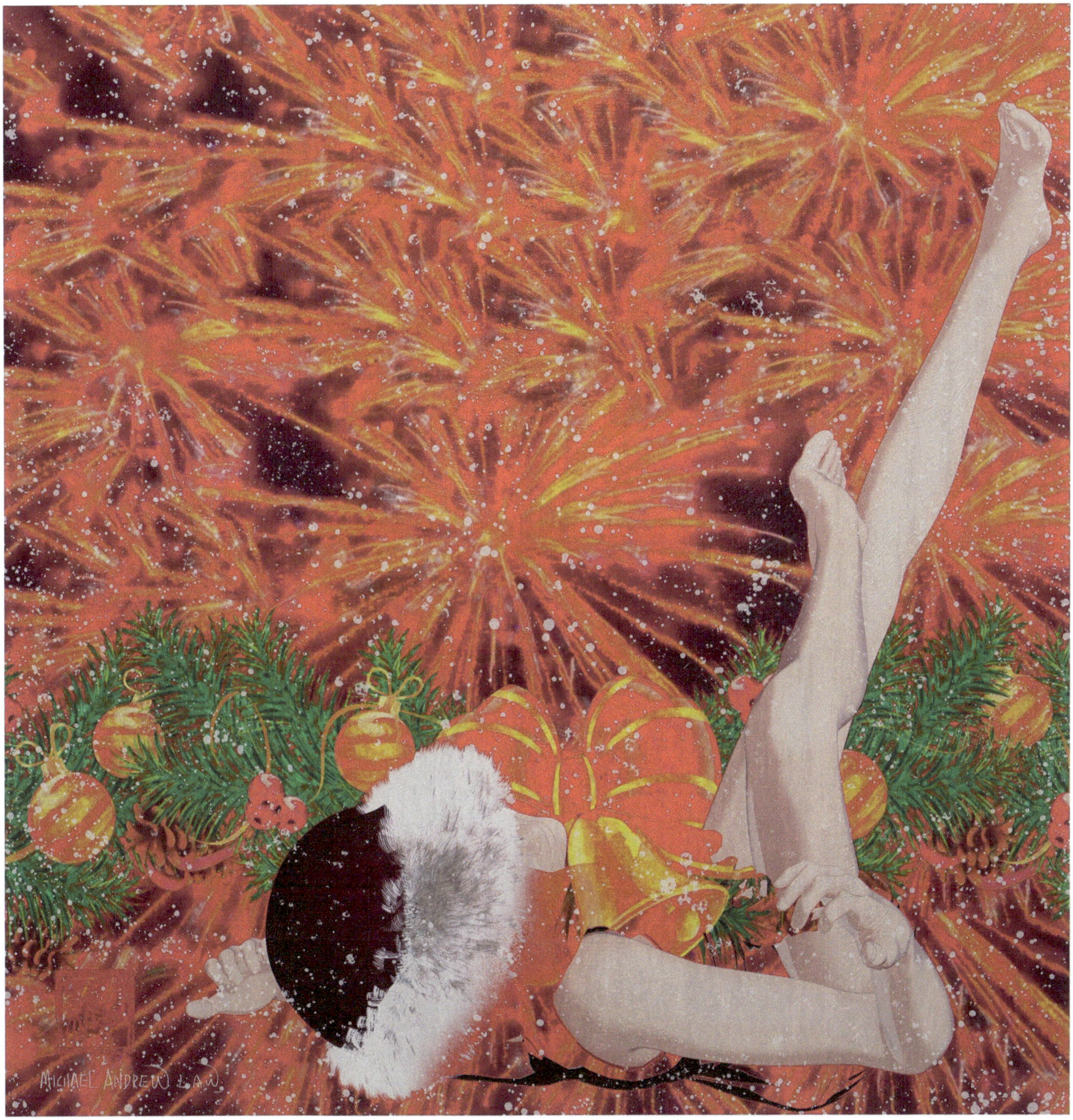

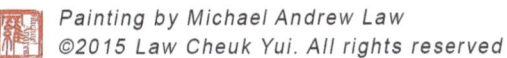

Christmas is not as much about opening our presents as opening our hearts

PLATE No.

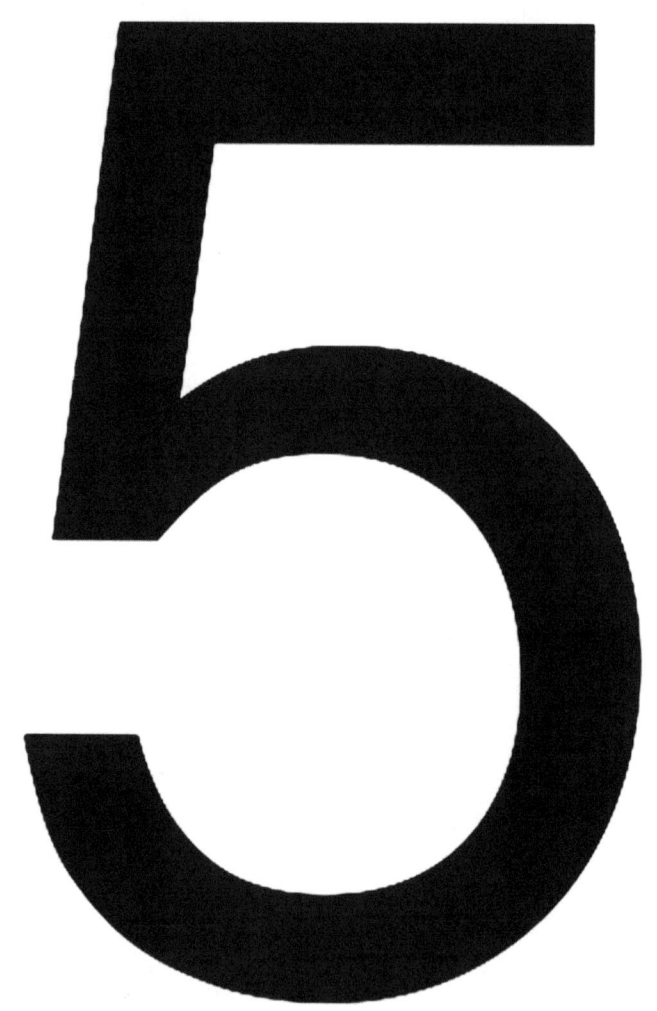

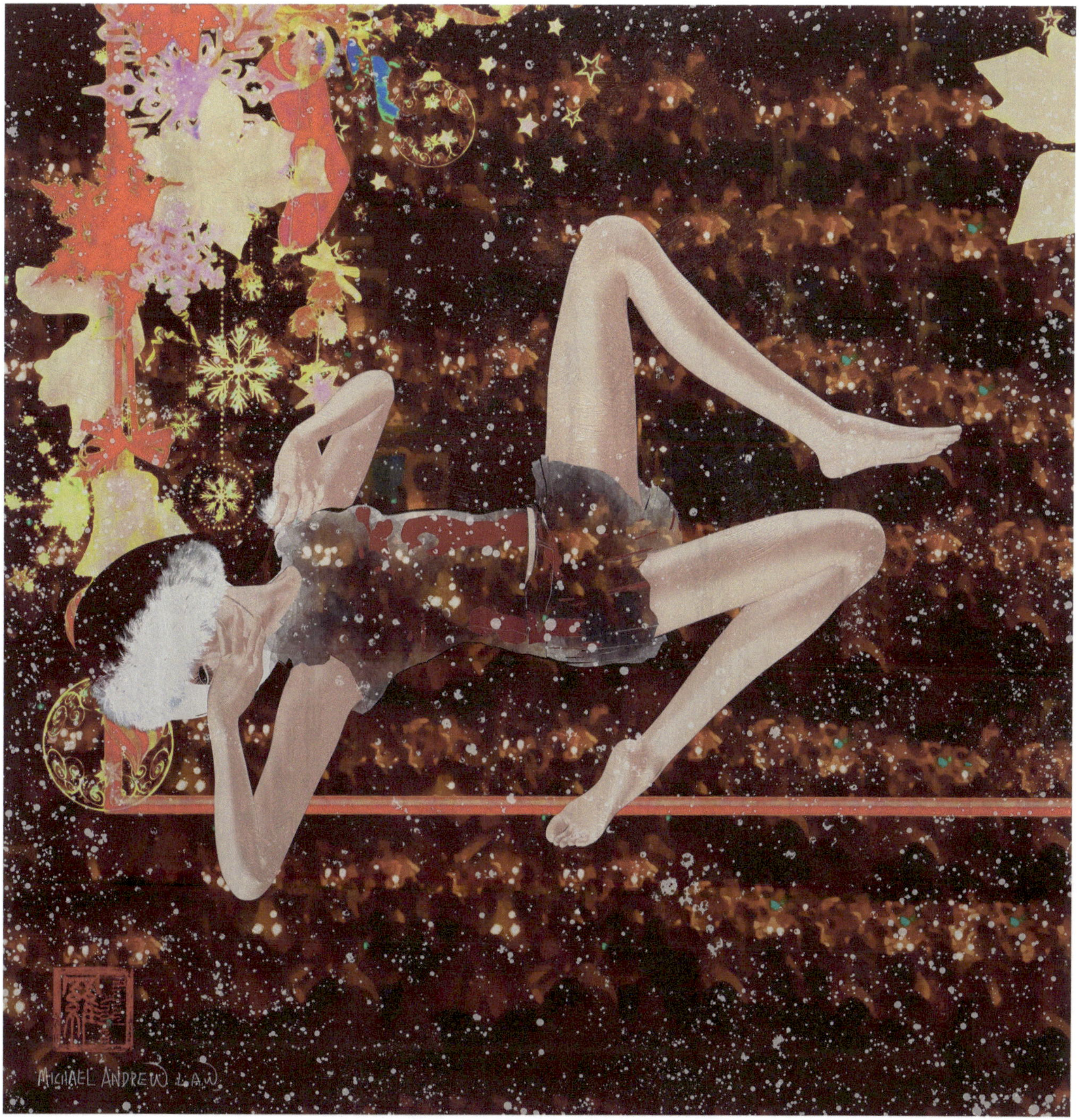

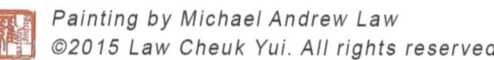

For the spirit of Christmas fulfils the greatest hunger of mankind

Painting by Michael Andrew Law
©2015 Law Cheuk Yui. All rights reserved

PLATE No.

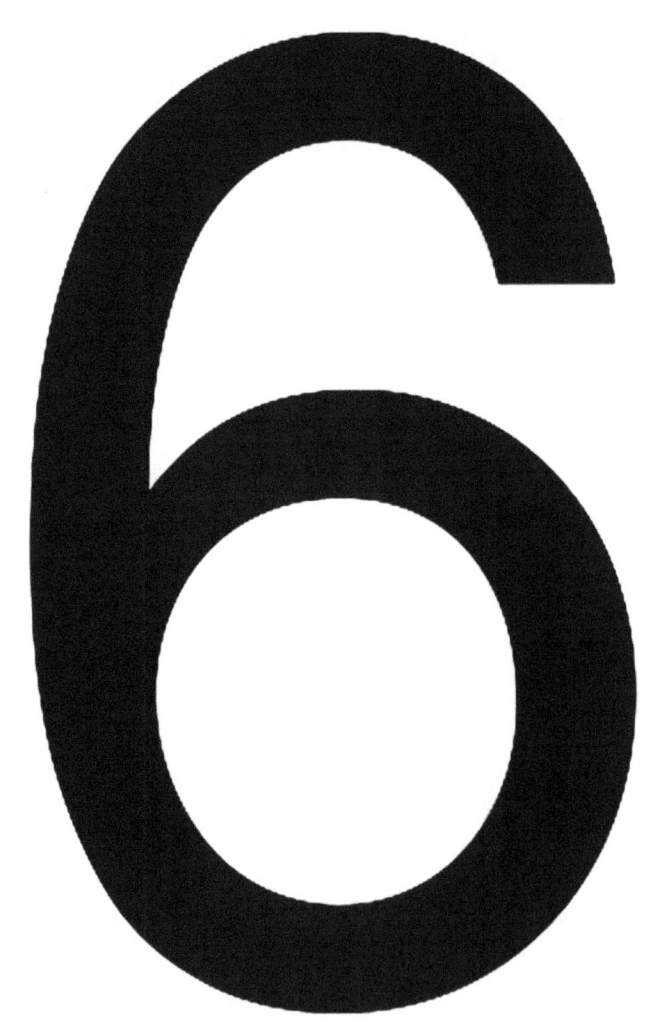

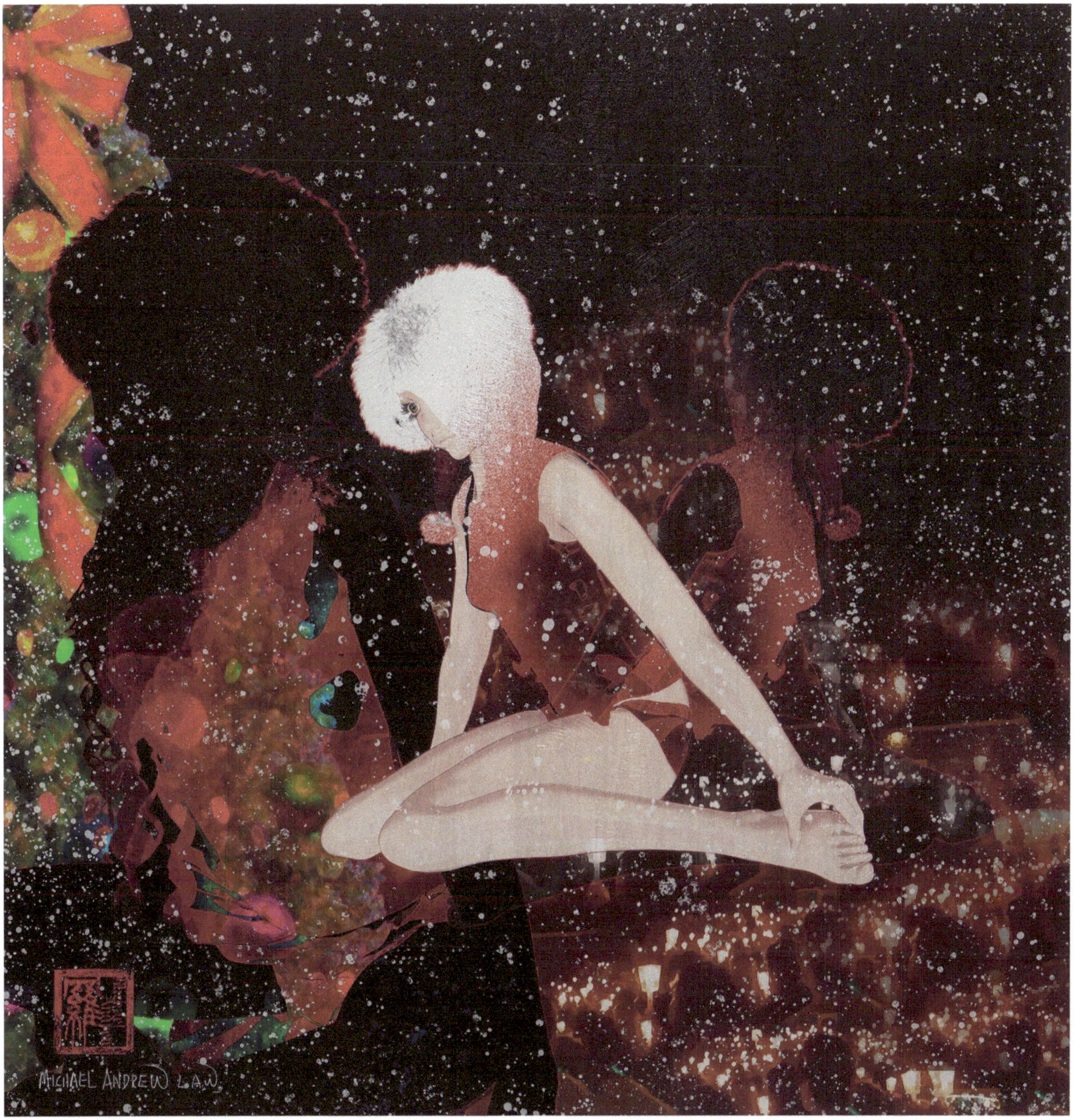

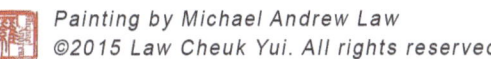

We are never alone

PLATE No.

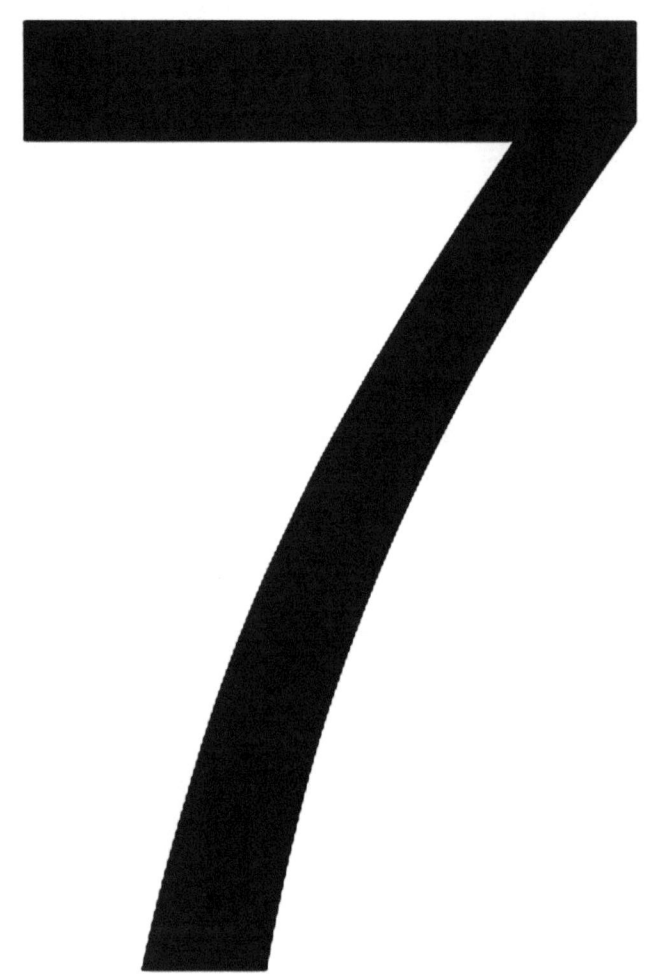

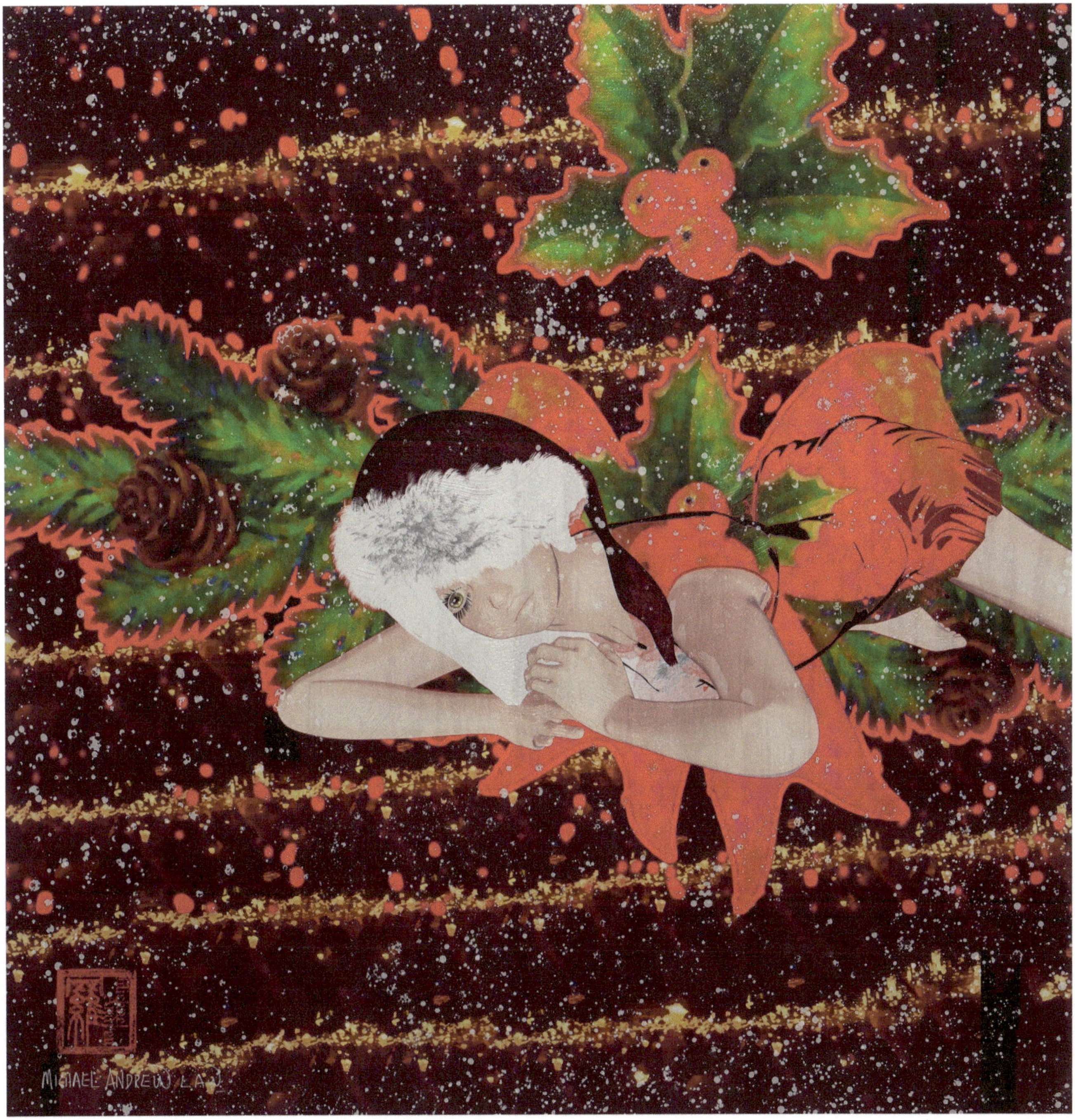

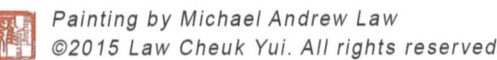

Rejoice and be happy

PLATE No.

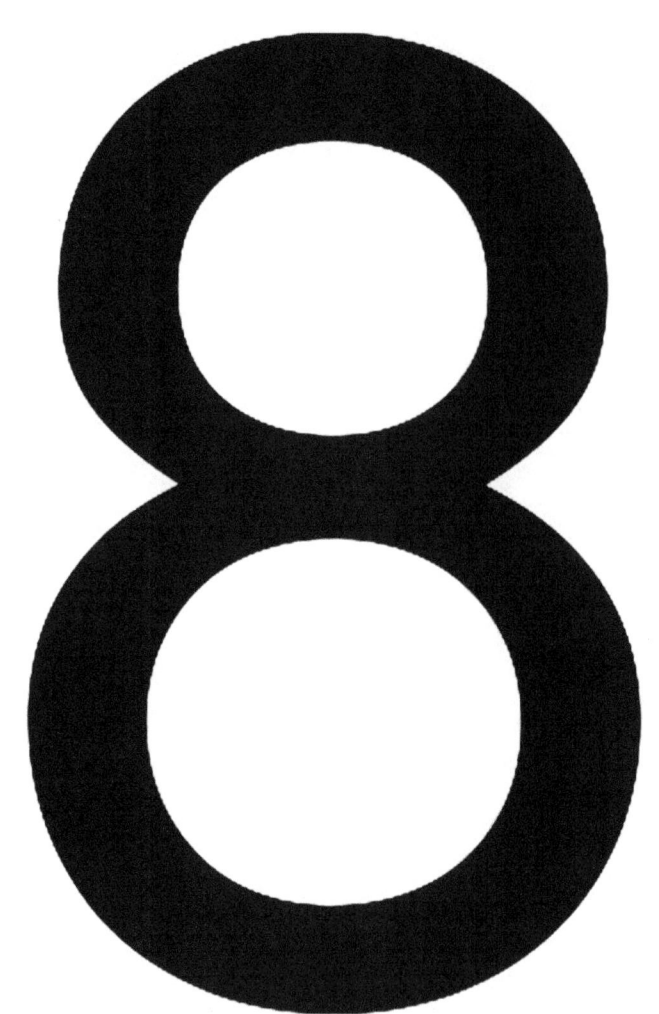

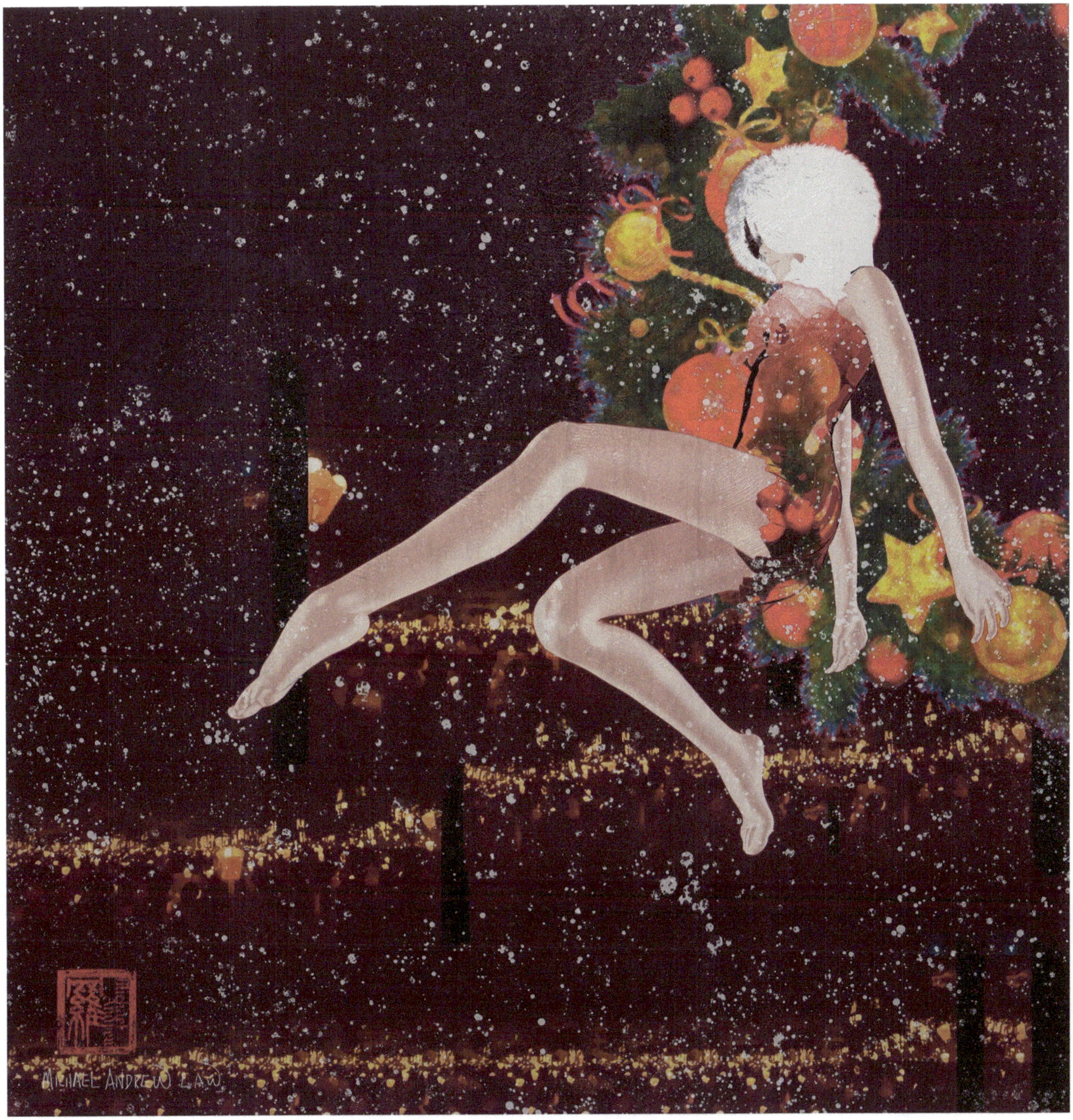

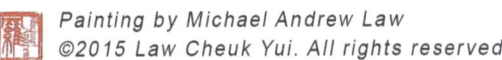

Peace, Joy and Love to you

PLATE No.

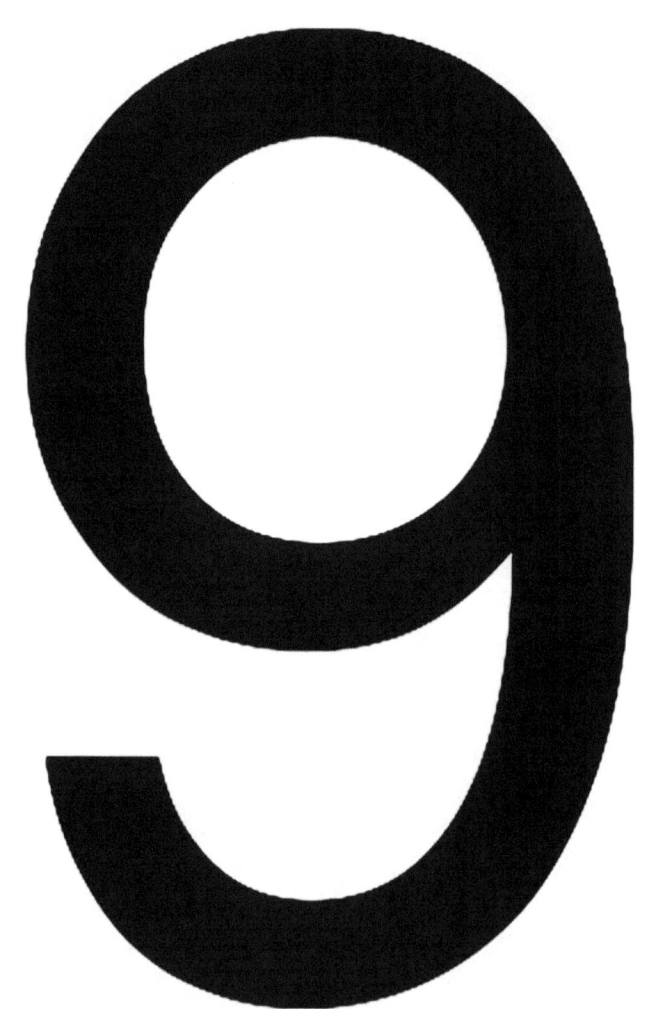

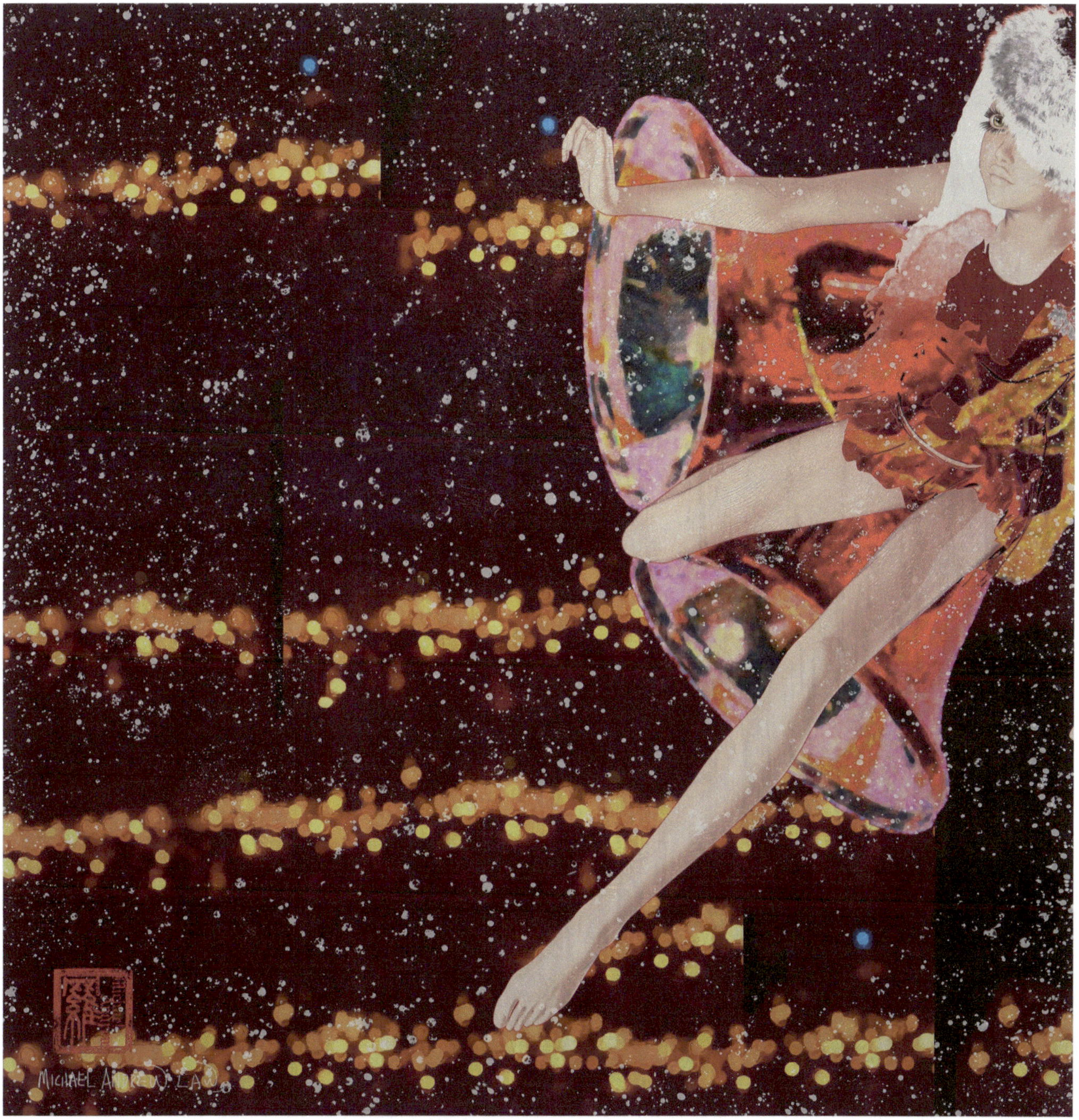

Have a warm and cozy Christmas

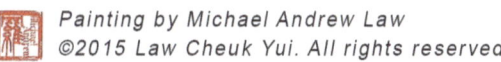

PLATE No.

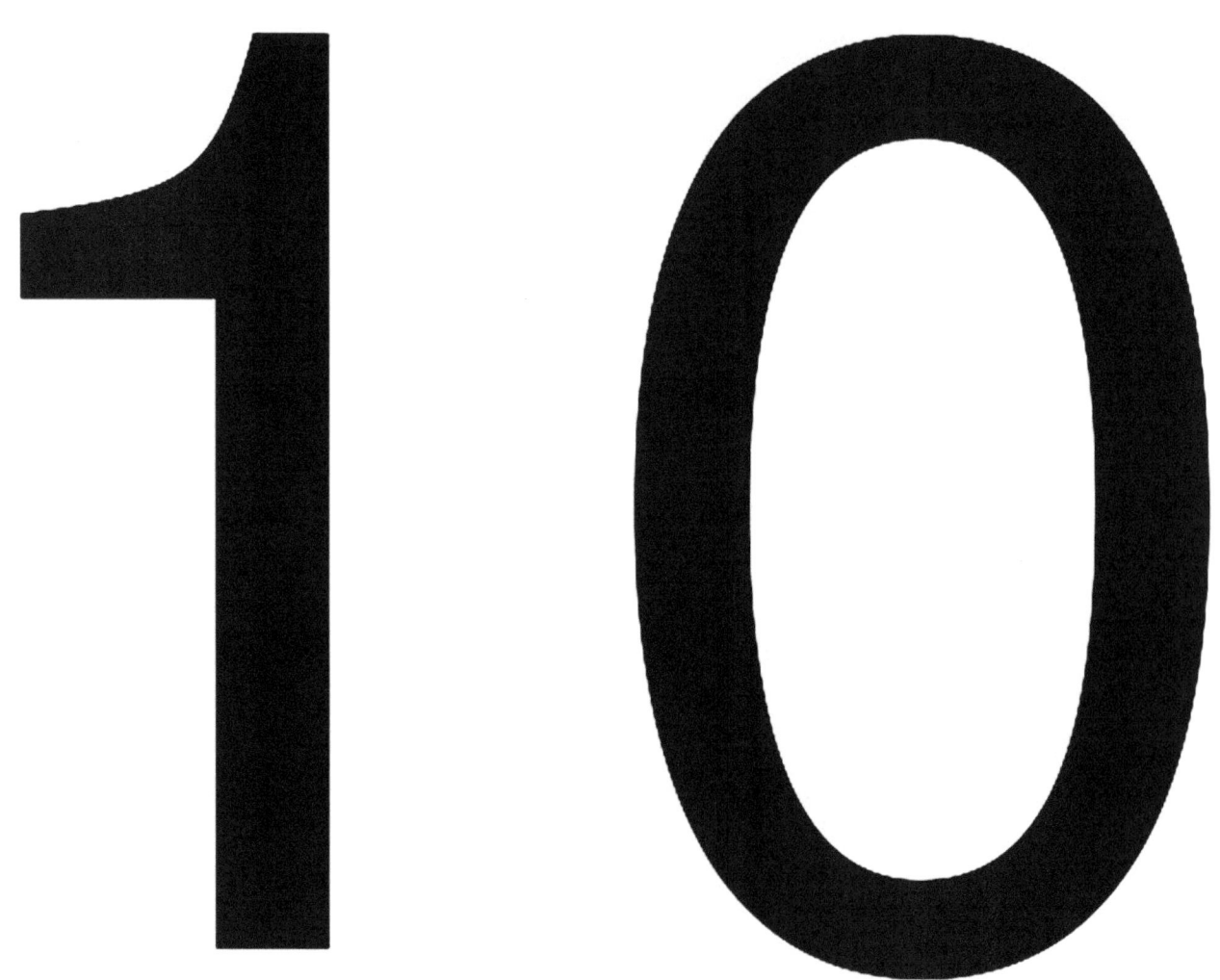

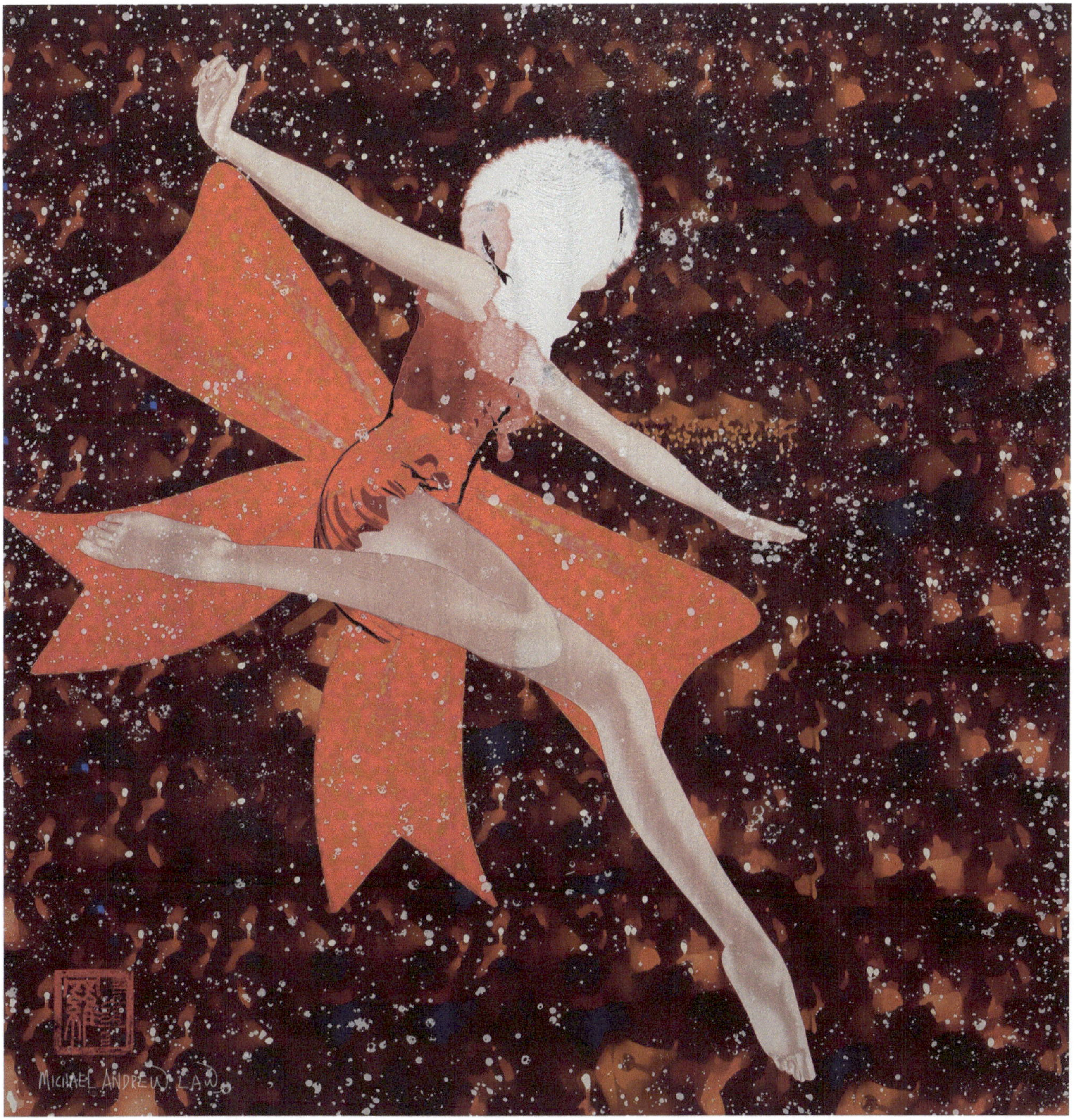

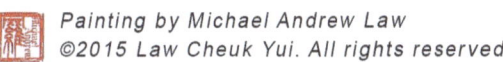

Peace on Earth and Joy to all

PLATE No.

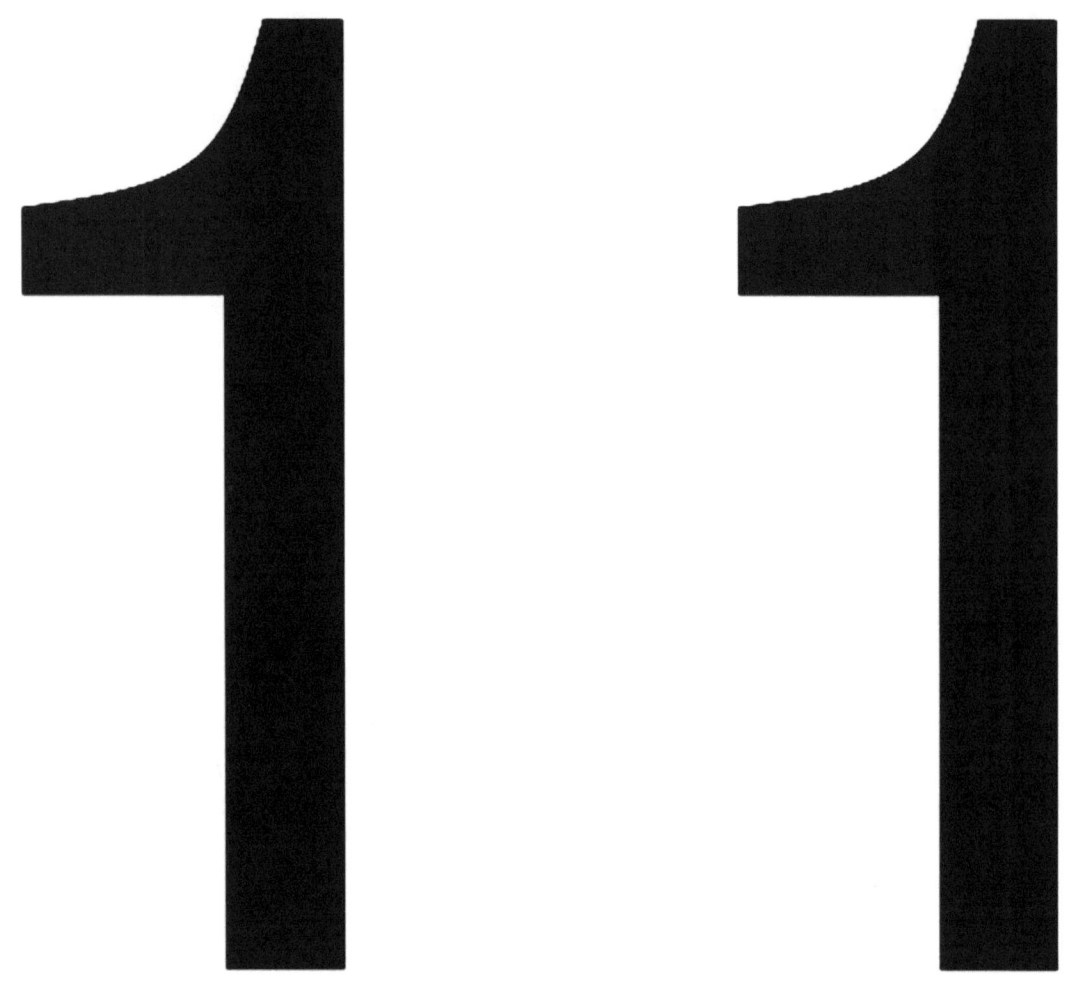

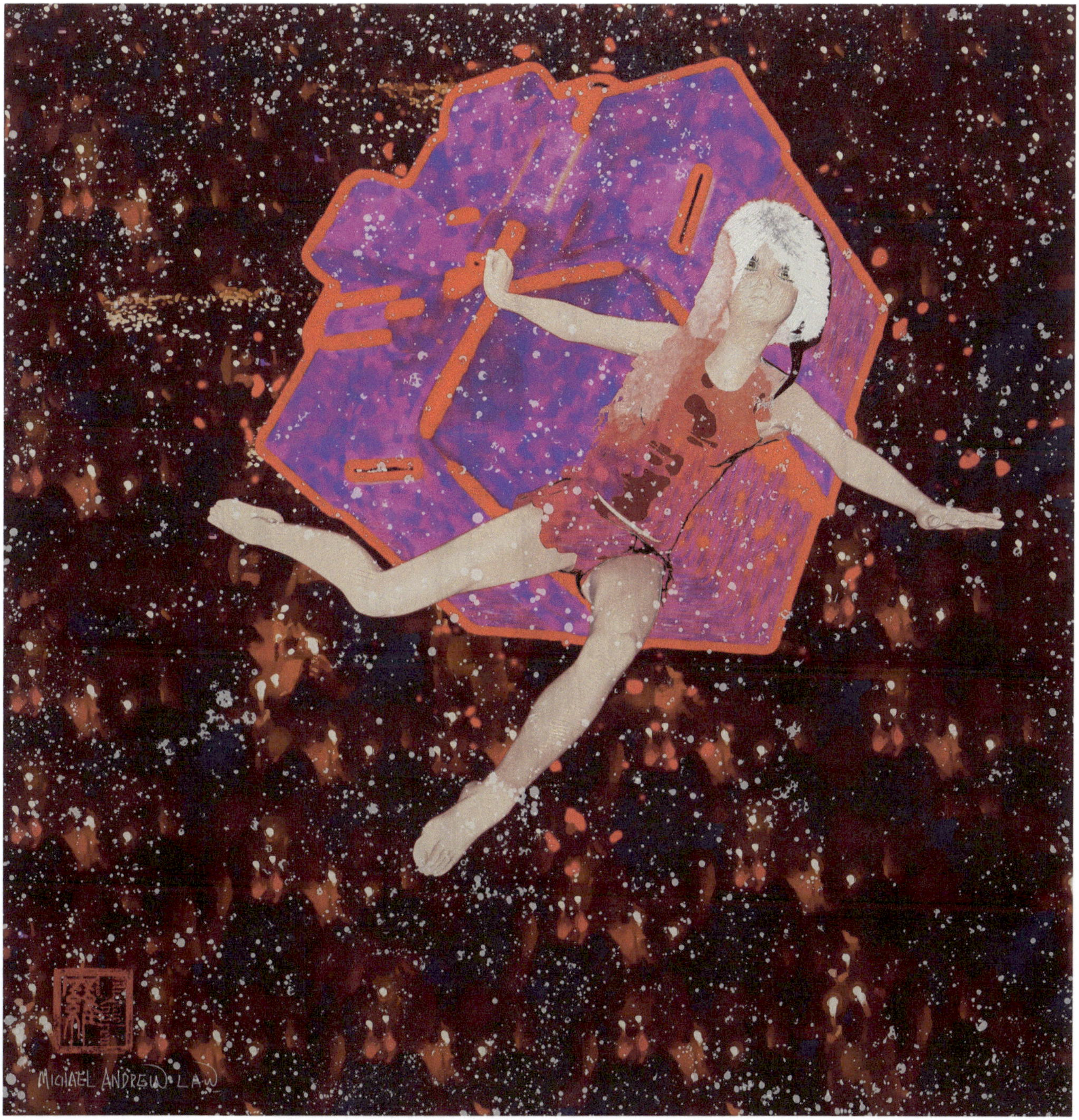

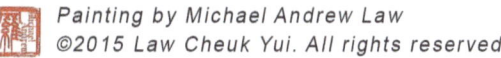

Wishing you a Christmas overflowing with Love and Laughter

Painting by Michael Andrew Law

PLATE No.

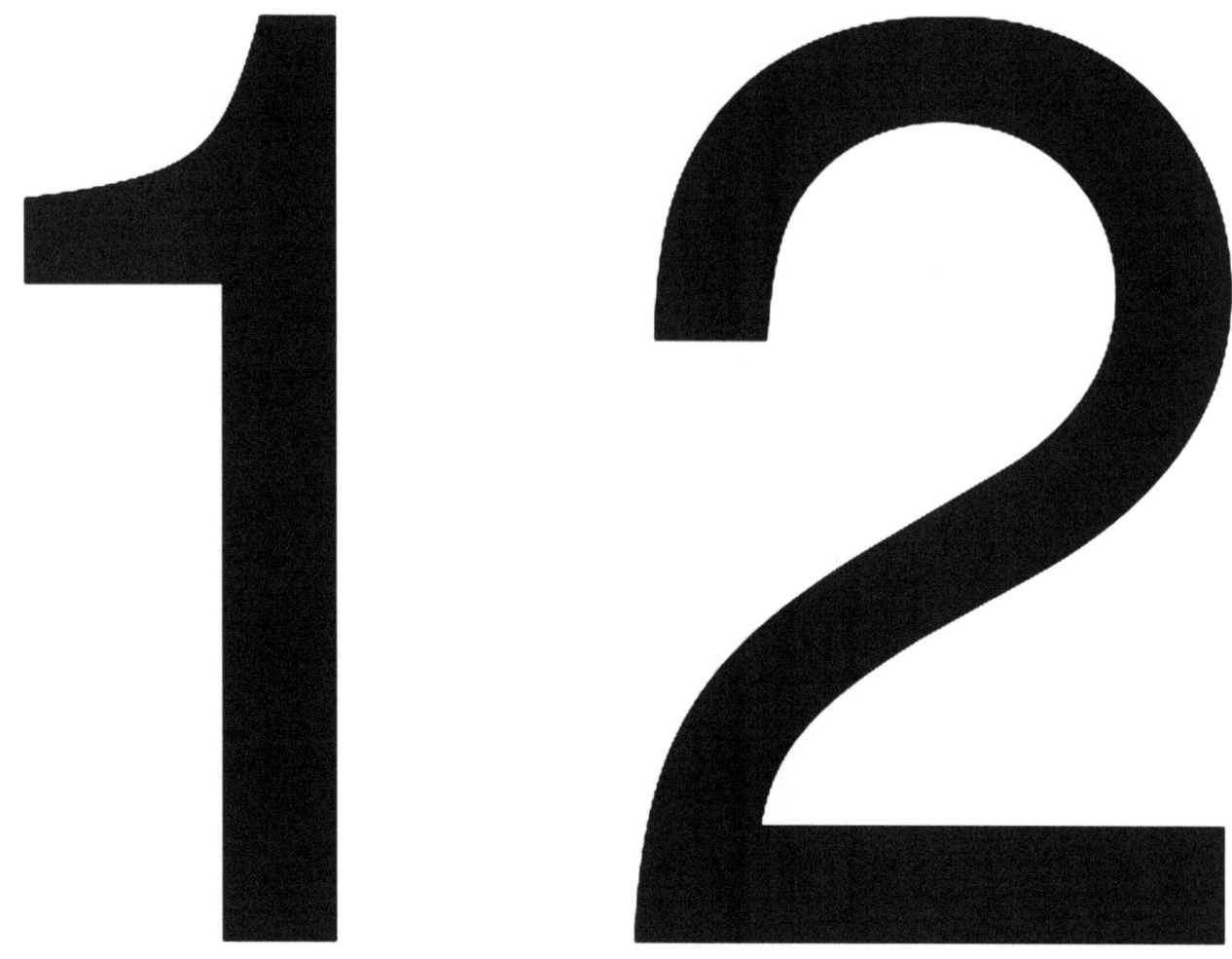

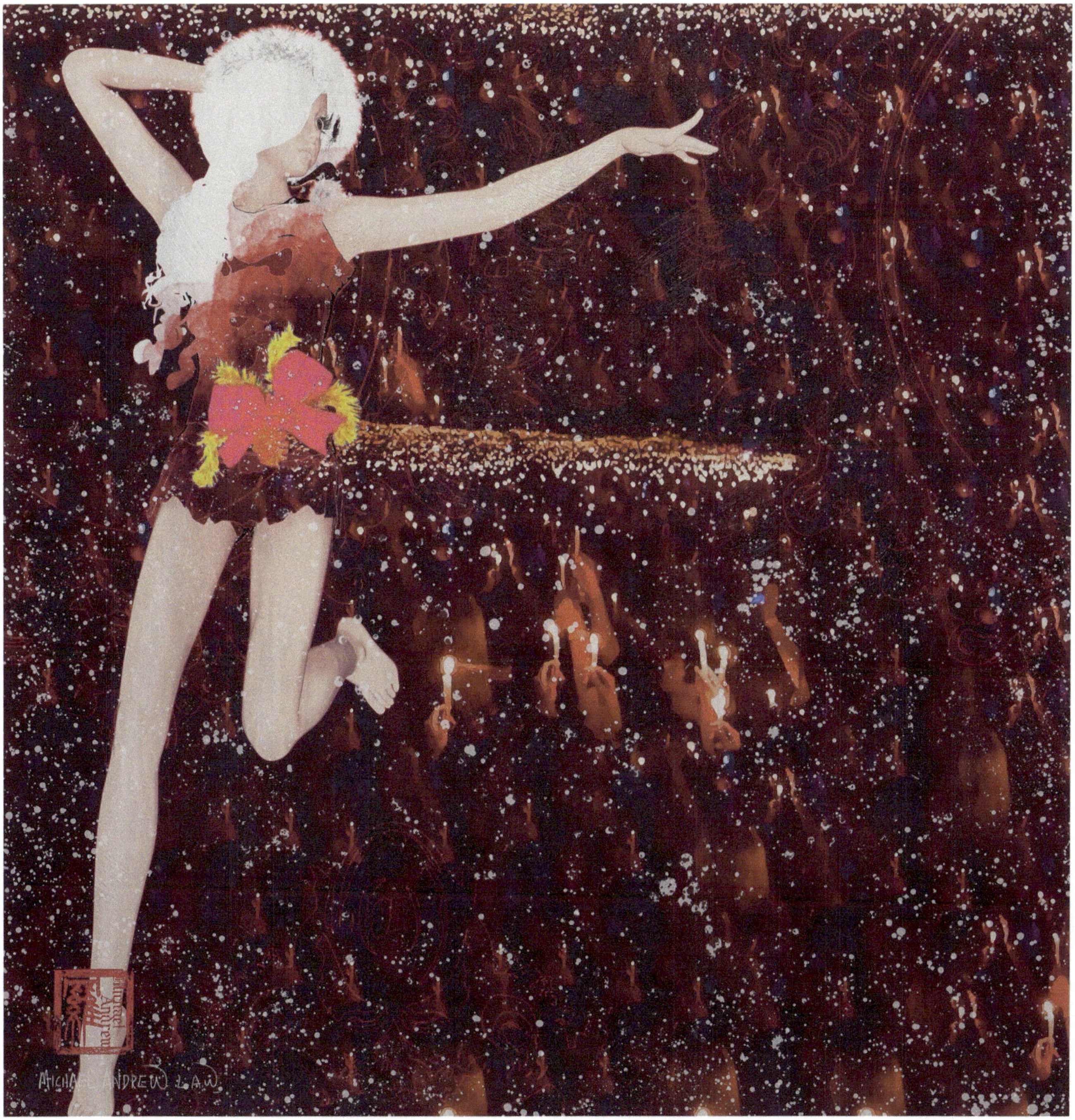

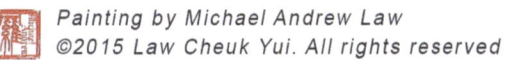

When we recall Christmas past, we usually find that the simplest things

PLATE No.

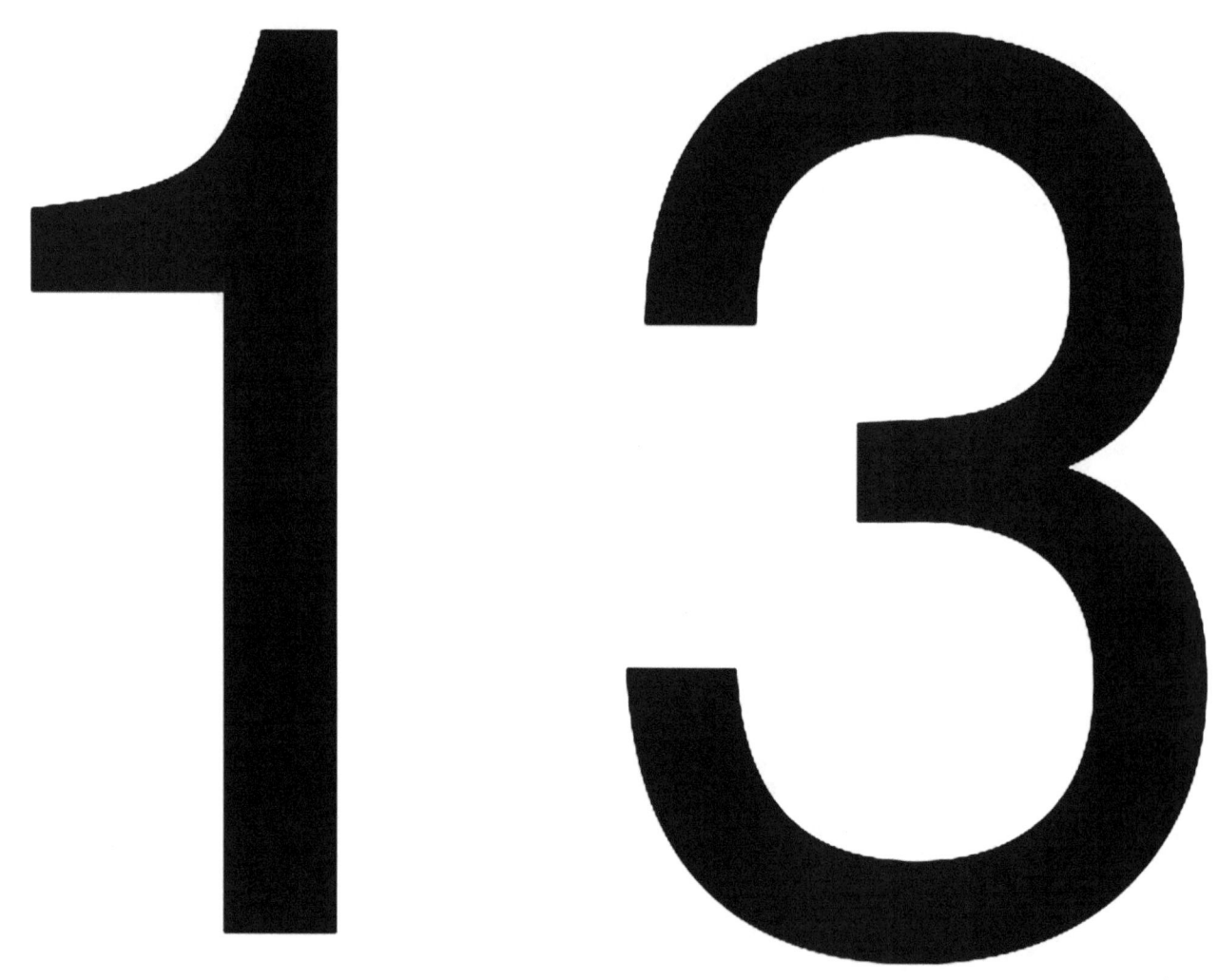

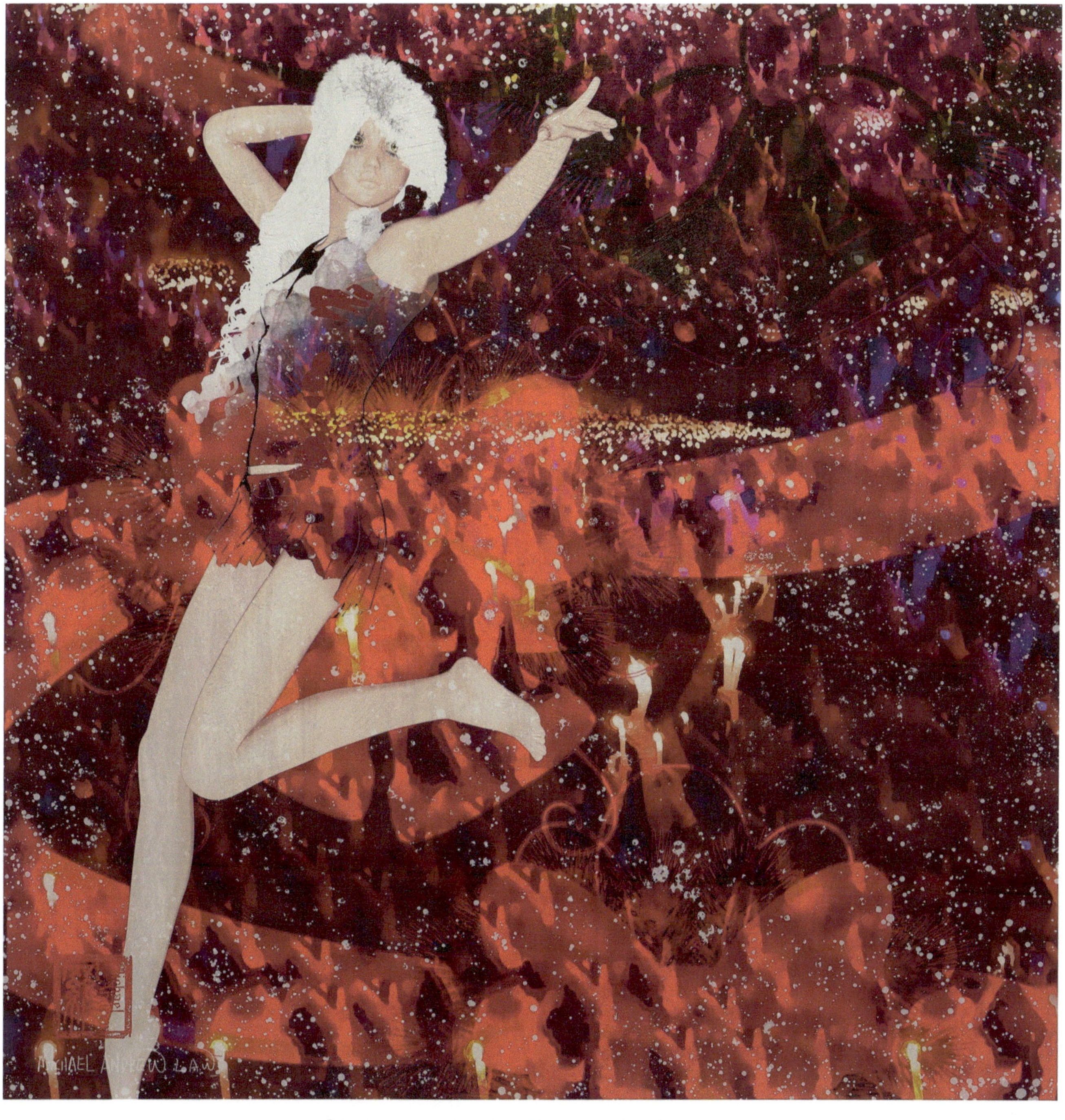

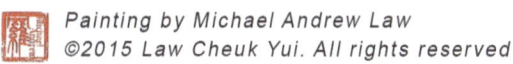

Christmas is the time to be home

PLATE No.

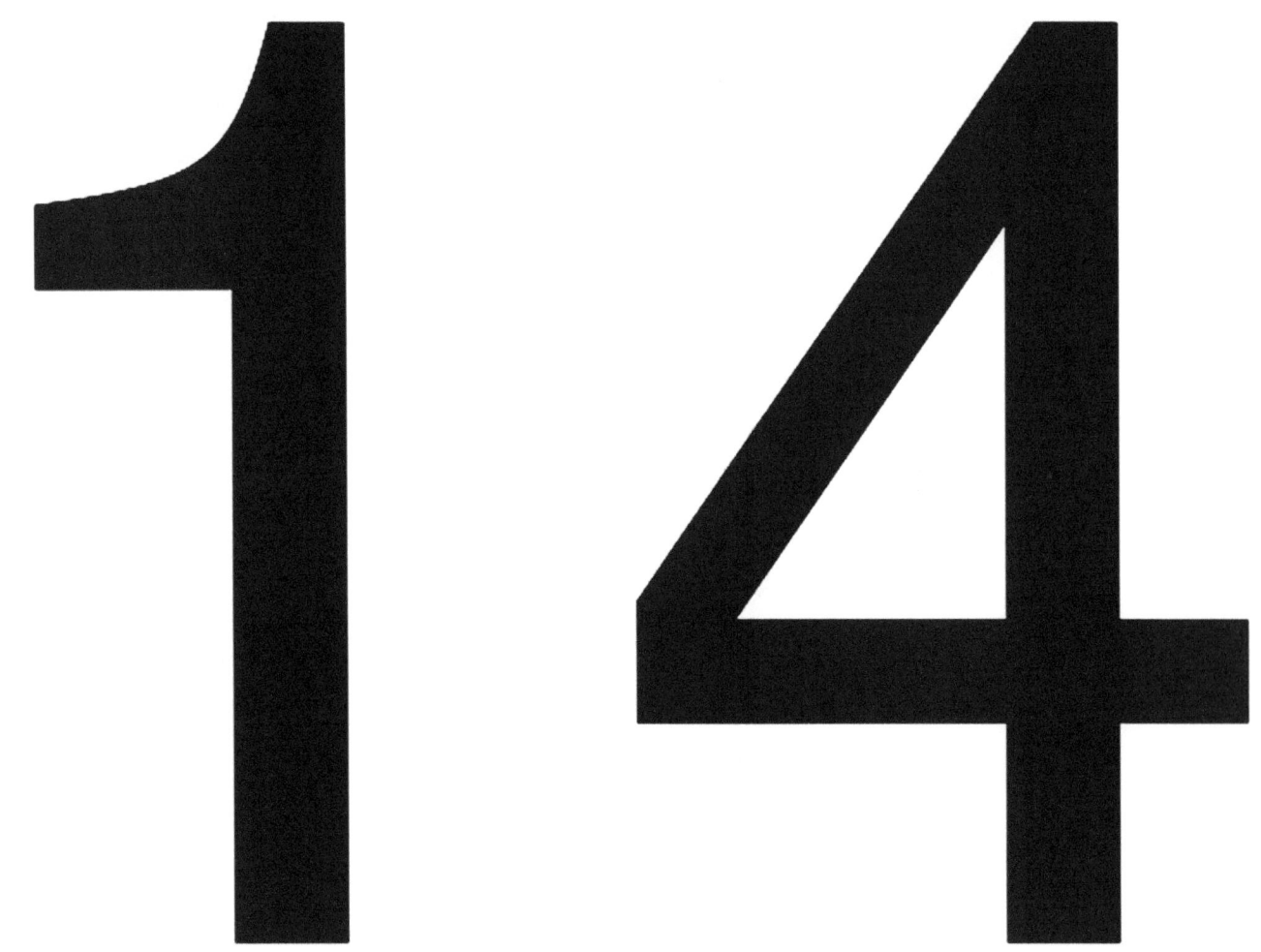

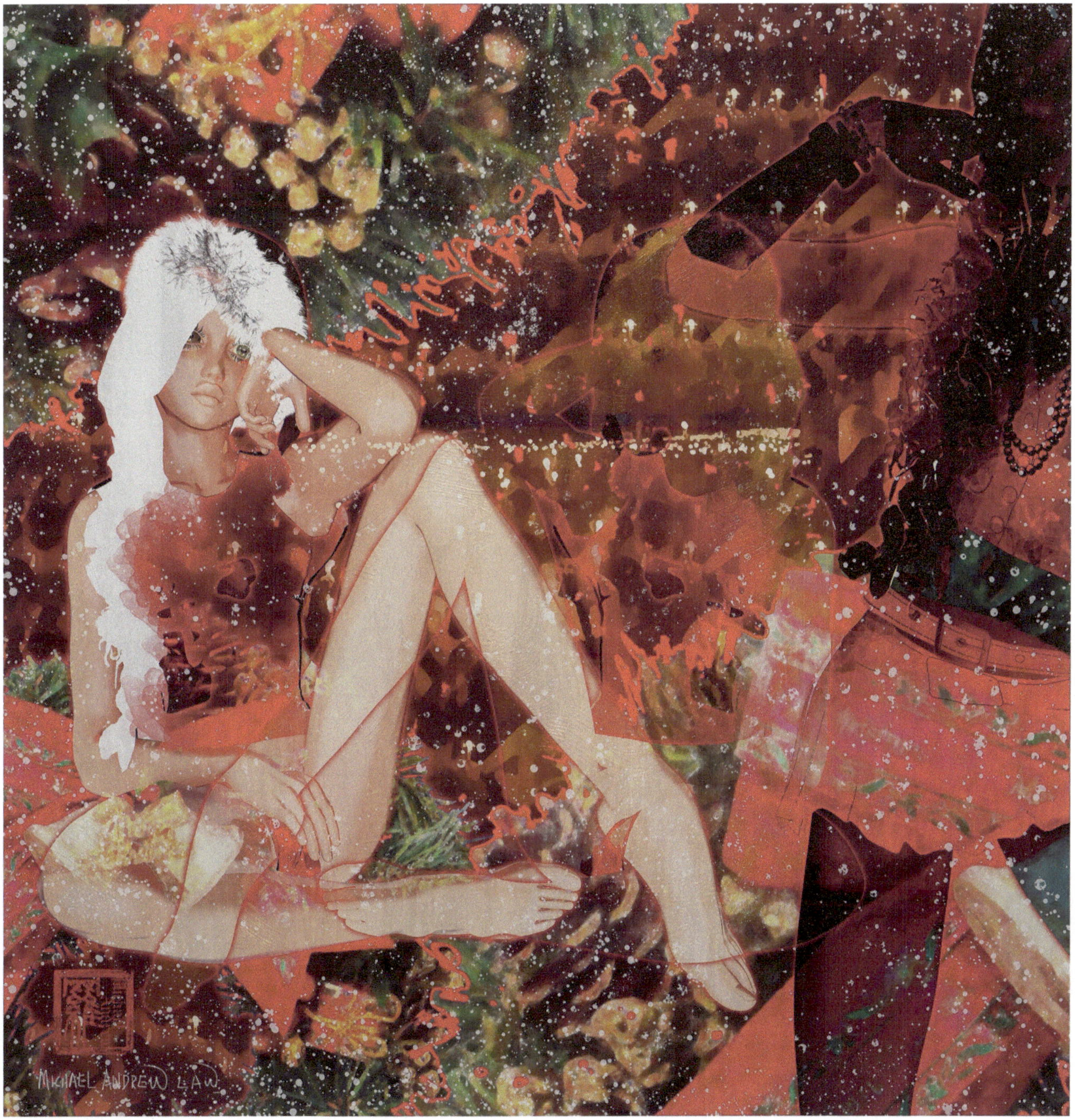

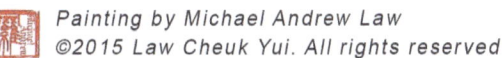

This is proved by what we feel in our hearts at Christmas

PLATE No.

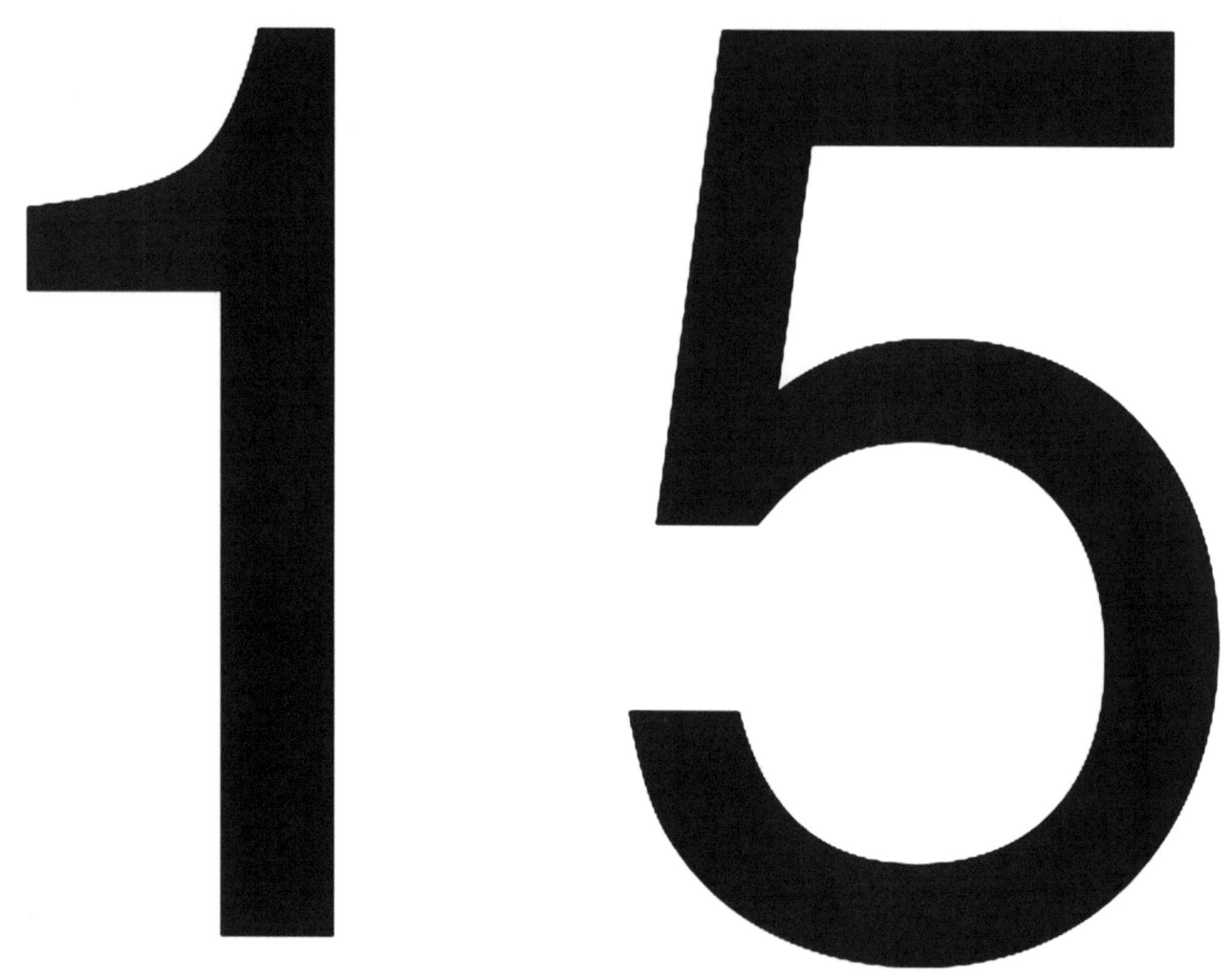

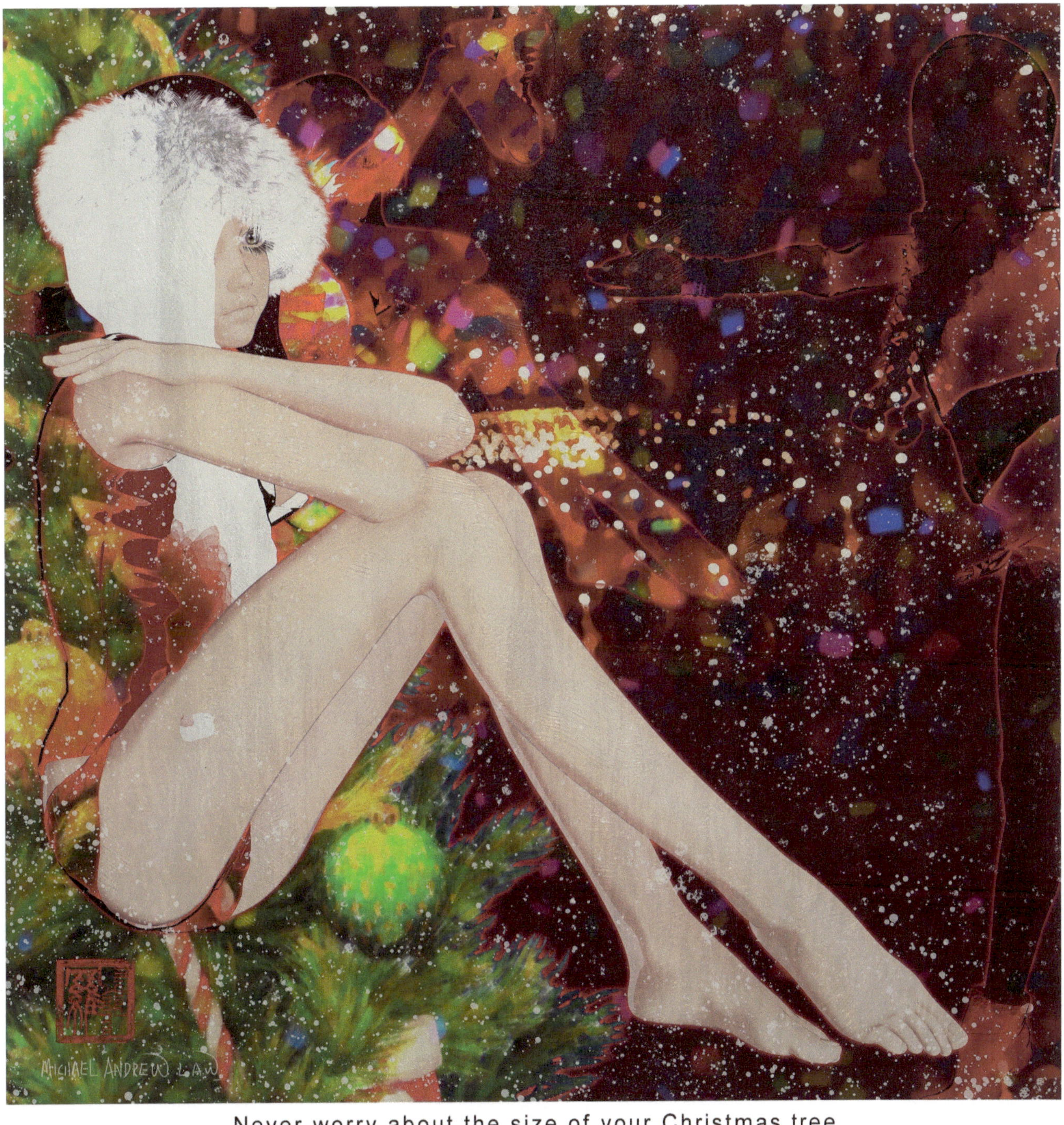

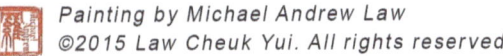

Never worry about the size of your Christmas tree

PLATE No.

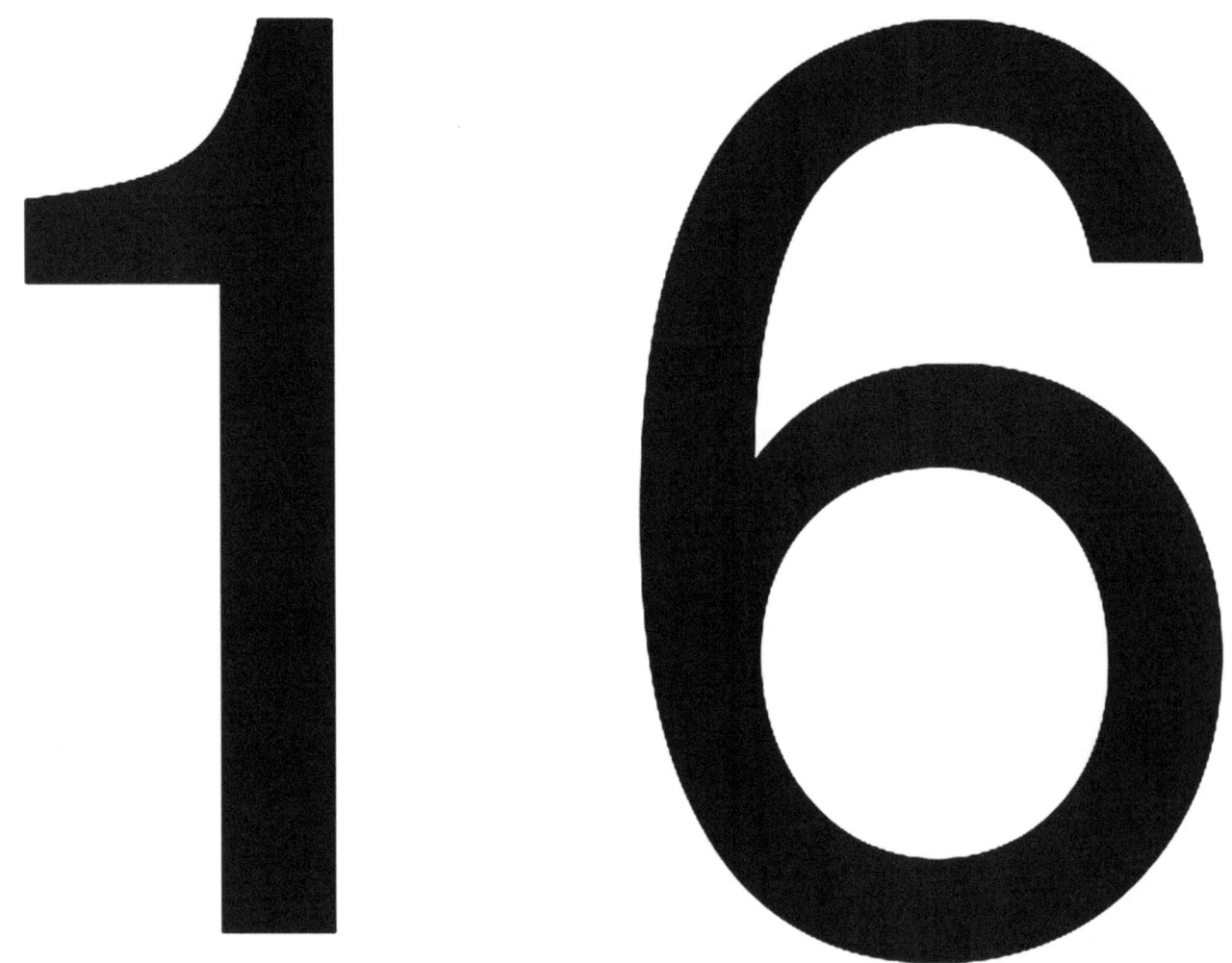

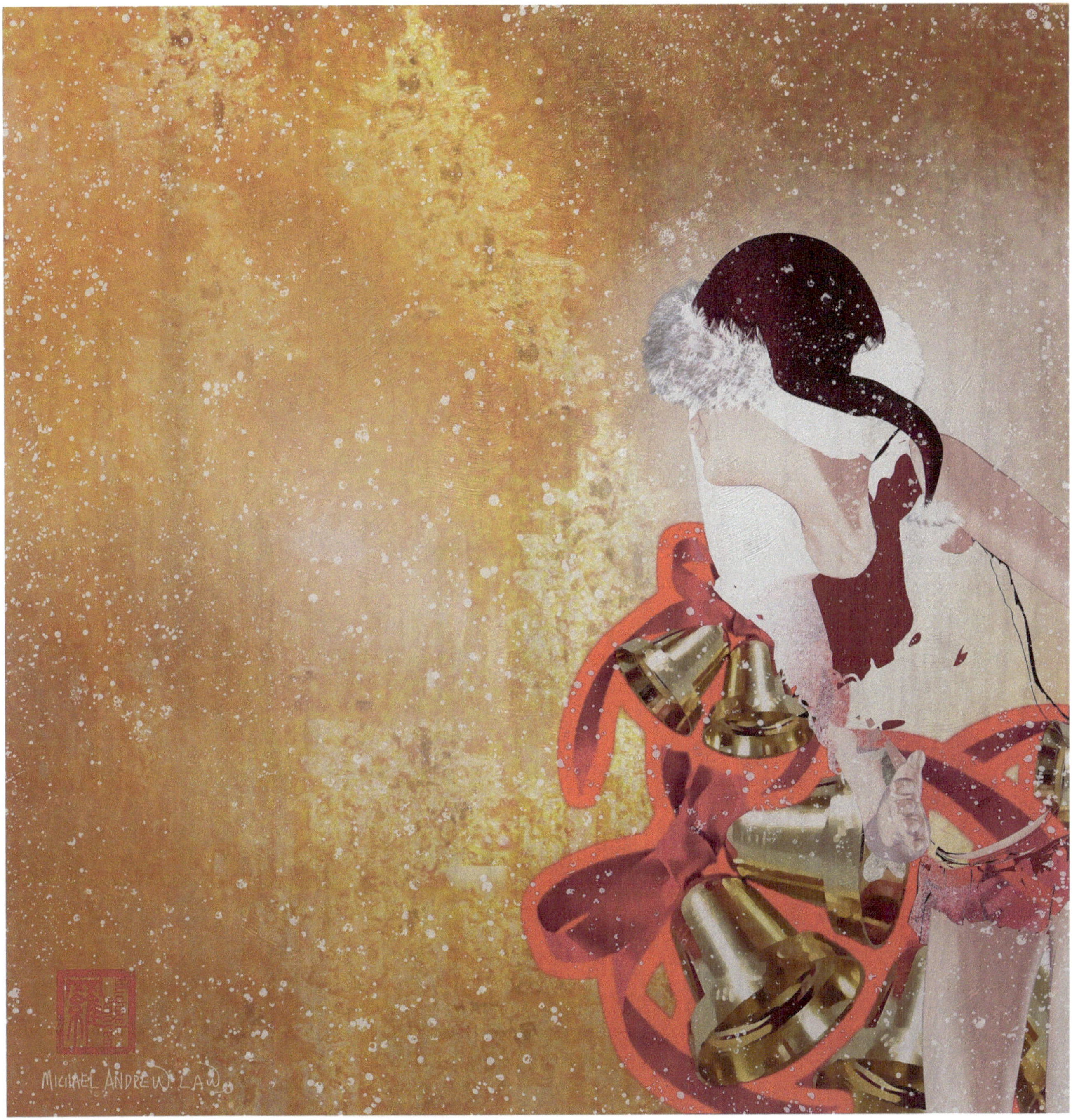

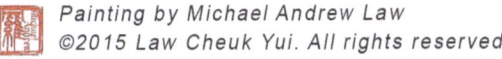

Christmas is the keeping-place for memories of our innocence

PLATE No.

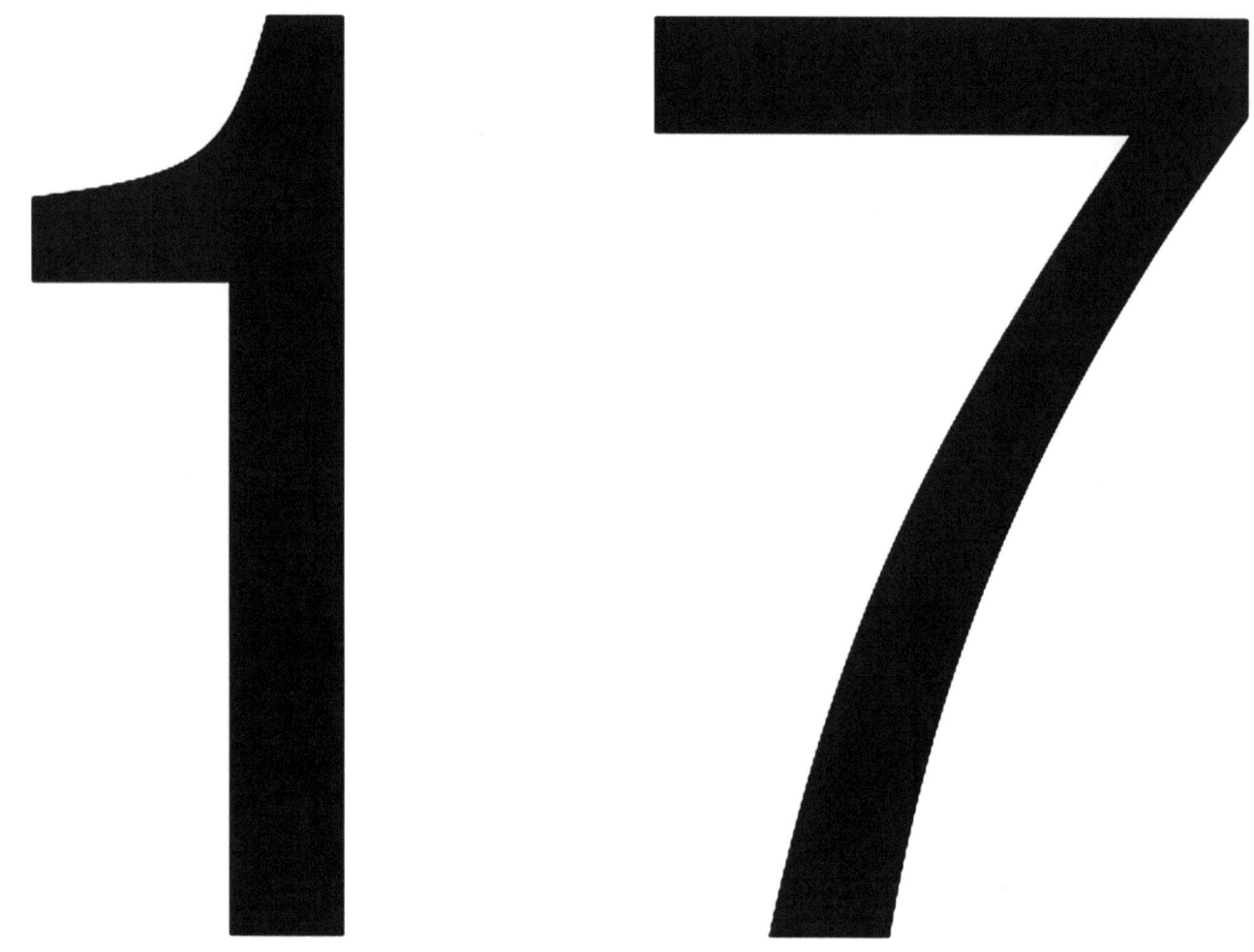

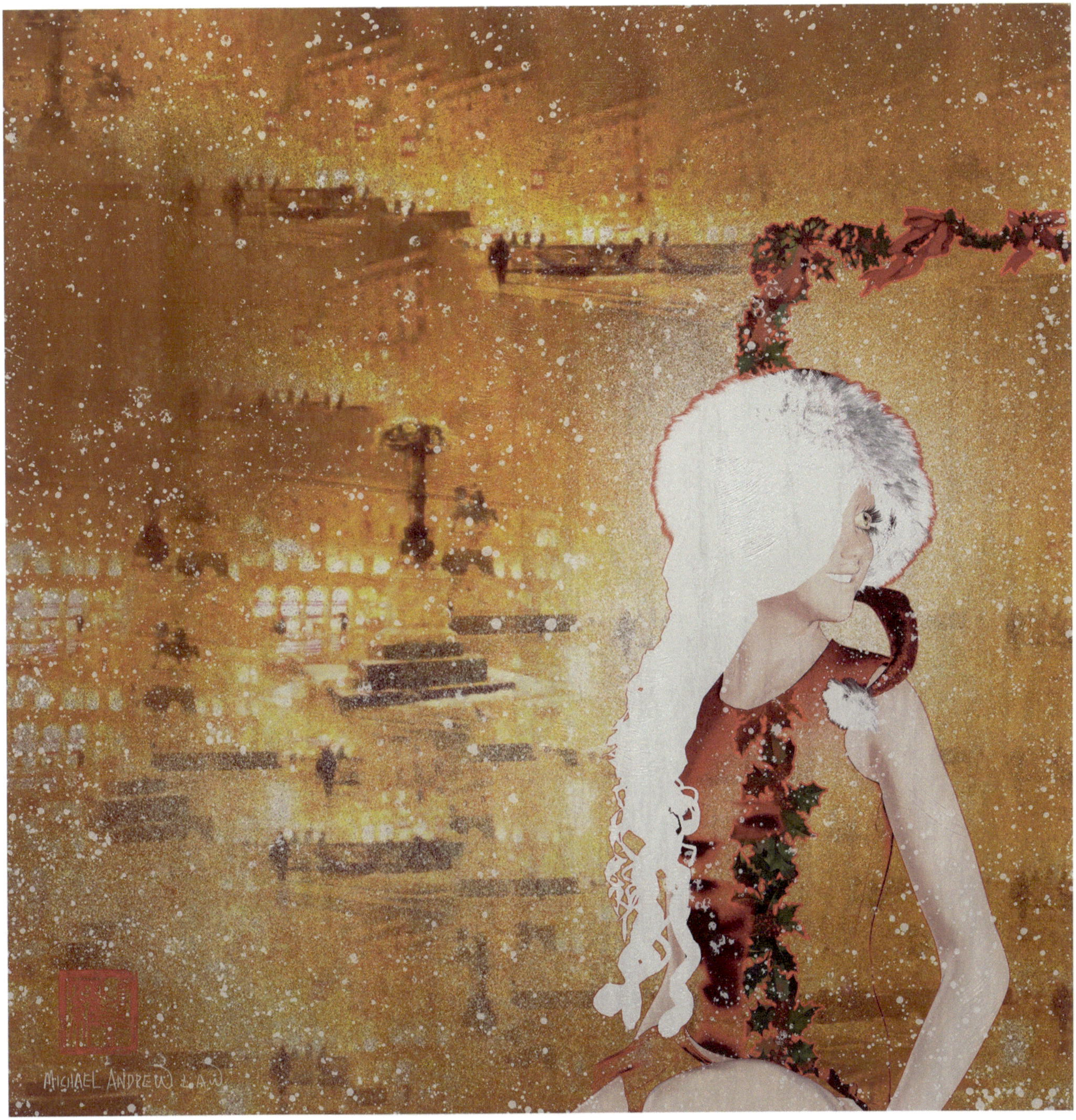

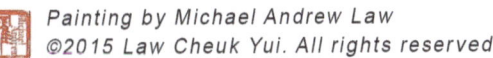

To be happy is the greatest wish in life

PLATE No.

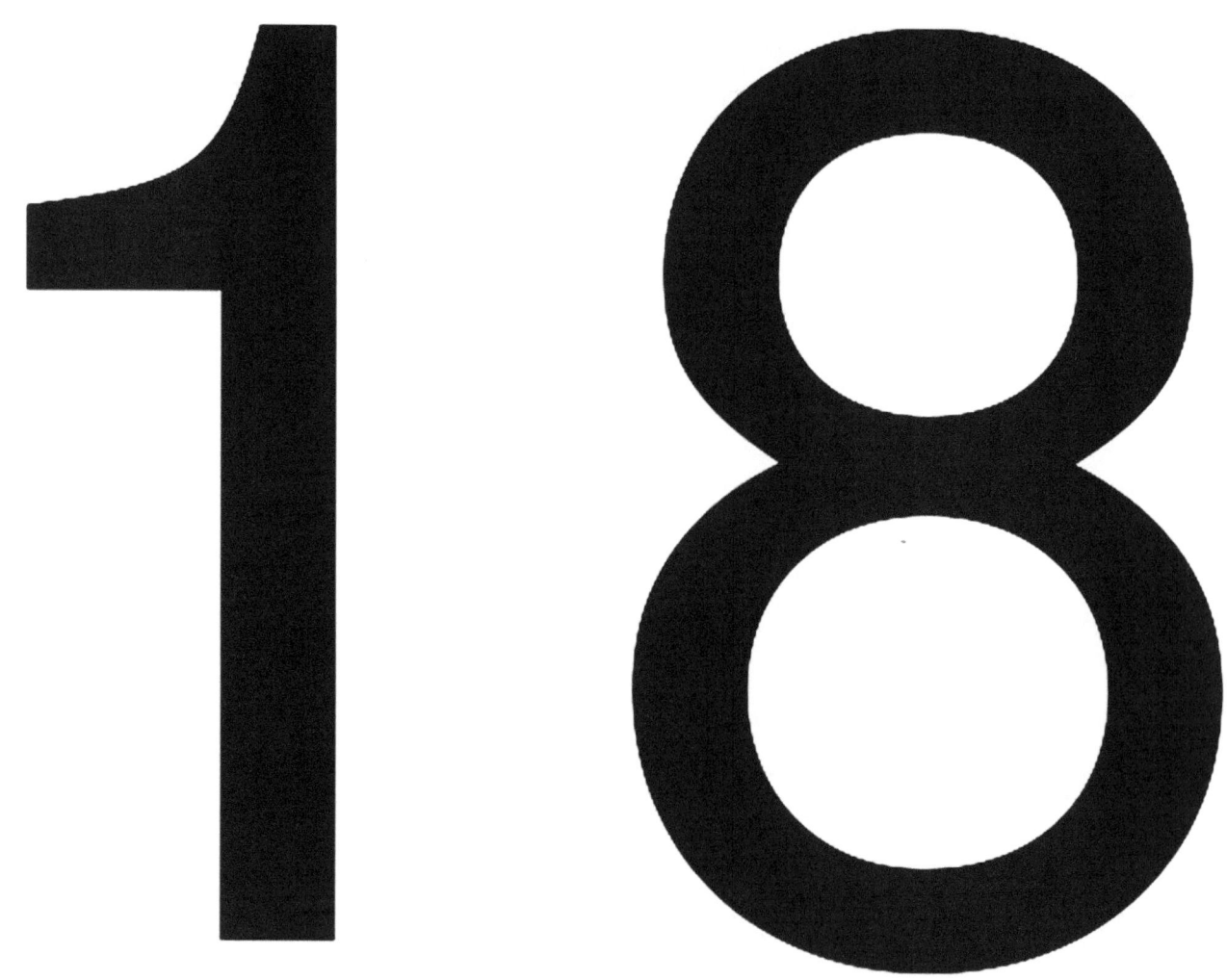

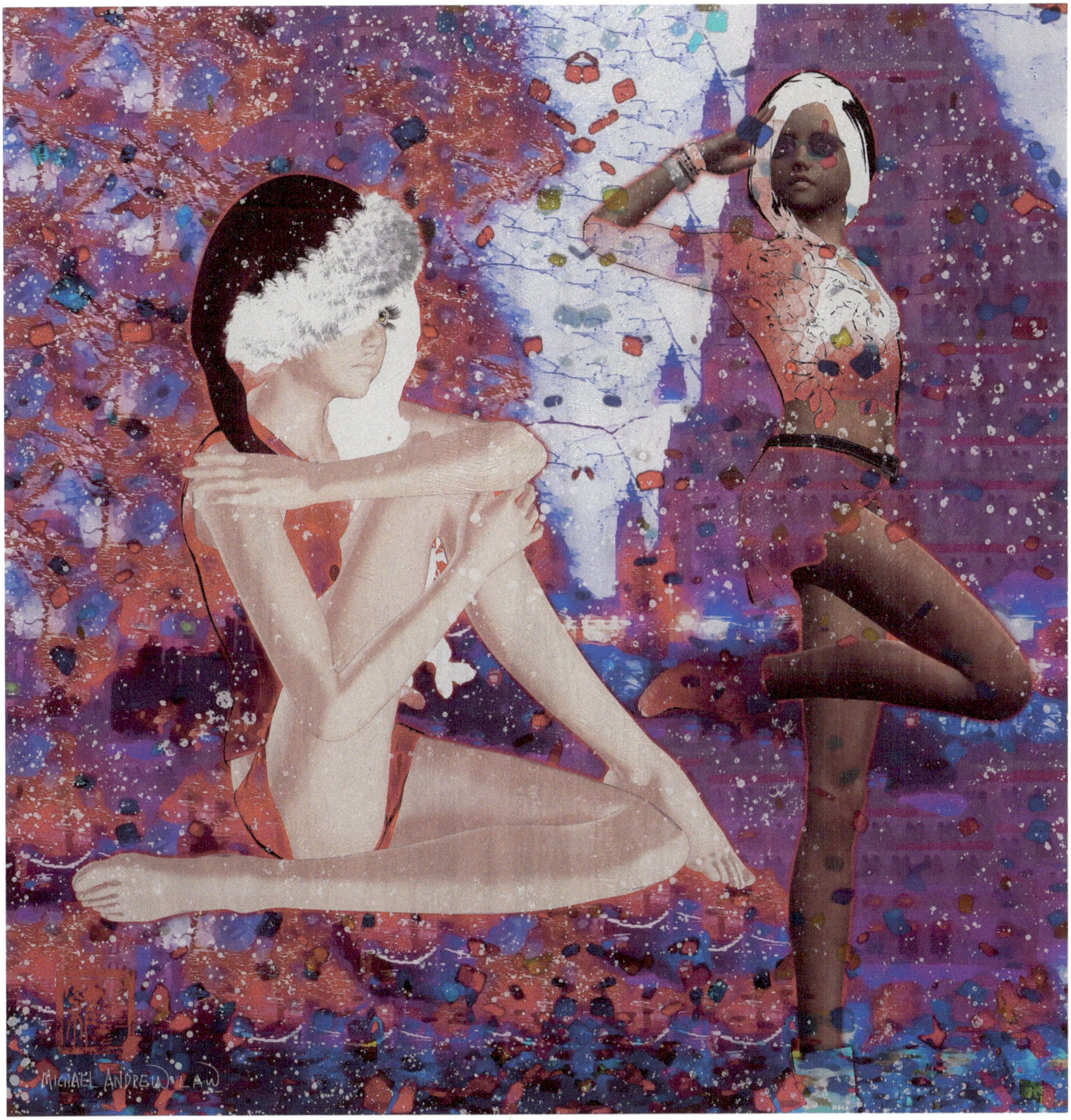

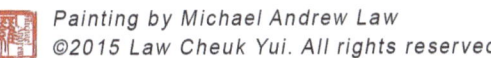

Blessings and peace of mind that you truly deserve

I really appreciate your purchase of Christmas Everyday Painting Collection , I hope you enjoy reading them as much as I enjoyed painting them!

May God bless your home with peace, joy and love. Have a merry Christmas!
By Michael Andrew Law.

Find Me Online.

Michael Andrew Law 🔍

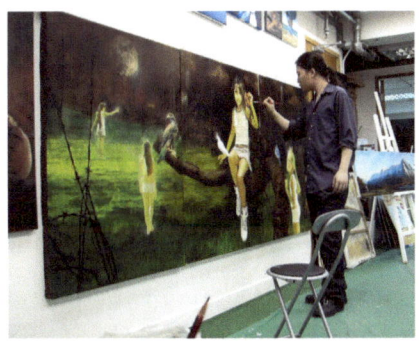

Michael Andrew Law at Work.

Michael Andrew Law fusing digital and classical painting with west and East creative philosophy , to produce an extremely original artistic language and content that bridged west and east ,classical and modern medium , at the same time clearly tells the stories of his own generation. Combining digital creative materials and classical painting techniques with effusive yet knowing and precise focused , his paintings maintain a powerful tension between opposing aesthetic forces—expression and knowledge, control and spontaneity, savagery and wit, urbanity and primitivism—while providing satiric commentary on the oppressive realities of the predicament of Generation Internet, homegrown hongkonger's local-culture vesus Traditional Chinese culture, and The Hong Kong's post-handover history.

In his dynamically designed compositions, gracefully detailed figures and innocent faces are incise against fields that juxtaposed with portraits, chinese calligraphy, and sometimes cgi. The Pale Hair Girls Series (2006 - 2013) depicts realistic cold, icy-like young female figures surrounded by abstract and expressively painted forms and shapes revealing images of Pop culture, Historial figures, and Hong Kong landmarks.

Michael Andrew Law draws inspiration from Old Master's works such as Caravaggio , Ruben , Rembrandt , all the way to the Modern Art Superstars such as Warhol , Lichtenstein , Richter , De Kooning , Bacon , Wool and Prince . The Pale Hair Girls series mainly inspired by the painting works of French academic painter and traditionalist William-Adolphe Bouguereau and the Late Great YiFei Chen's characteristic "Romantic Realism" paintings.

In a reversal of standard East-West aesthetics, Law re-interprets Old Master's sophisticated imagery combine classical and digital materials—which resonate with Digital Vector Designs and Paintings—with fine strokes of oil paint multi-layered with paint film.In his interpretation of Leonardo Da Vinci's iconic Mona Lisa's smile (1517)—an iconic image that has been endlessly disseminated and reproduced—Law painted over the symbolism of the portrait Mona Lisa with his young wife , intent on rendering the figure in contemporary fashion with the iconic image as background .

"The Humanity triptych" depicts New Generation HongKongers in a Ruined Hong Kong city , awaiting their unknown fate of a new beginning. This painting series explores one of the central paradox of his art—between romance and derision , his romantic magnanimity as an artist and his pessimistic perspective on the predicament of Generation Y Hongkongers. Here, this paradox is symbolized by the stark contrast of icy cold young female and disturbing representations of the armageddon-like of images. Whether portrayed as single "chinese calligraphy " or in triptych composition and classical paintwork that combine both expressive and traditional painting techniques with the digital vector , the beauties and the human figures stand as eternal motifs in the history of art and also in popular culture. Both oppositional and parallel, they are reminders of the fragile vibrancy of life and the impitoyable passing of time.

A references between different cultural refrence (high/pop, classical/contemporary, east/west), Michael Andrew Law has stated that an artist should be someone who understood how to hybrid between different worlds and go ahead makes an effort to knowing them. With his distinctive "iEgoism" philosophy , which employs highly refined academic painting techniques to depict a mixture of abstract expressionism within a representational pop culture images. These techniques parallel to the themes of romance and predicament of this generation , he recollects and revitalizes narratives of irony and introspection.

Michael Andrew Law was born in 1982 in British Hong Kong , studied fine art with american artist Daniel Anderson and with artist graduatee of China Central Academy of Fine Arts Sam Zeng from 2003 - 2006 . He co-founded the Hong Kong Art Studio Nature Art Workshop in 2008. In addition to the production and marketing of Michael Andrew Law's art and related work, Nature Art functions as a supportive environment for the
fostering of emerging Hong Konger artists. Law is also a curator. In 2013, he organized an exhibition of contemporary art titled "iEgoism ," which served as a commentaries of contemporary HongKong Gen Y pop culture ;These Theroy also published in the book : "ïEgoism" in 2014.

Michael Andrew Law currently works and lives in Hong Kong.

For further information please contact the studio at info@michaelandrewlaw.com or at +852.6444.7550. All images are subject to copyright. Artist/Studio/Gallery's approval must be granted prior to reproduction.

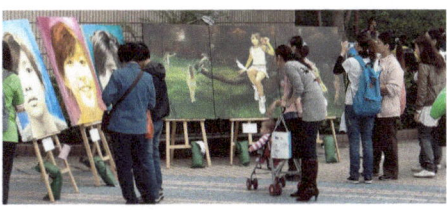

2010 Avenue of Stars, Hong Kong

Exhibition :

2013 DeTour Matters 2013 Satellite Events at NatureArt Gallery
2013 December to Remember , One man show at NatureArt Gallery Central District, Hong Kong.
2012 Solo Show , Park Central tseung kwan O ,Hong Kong
2011 Art Walk Group Showing , Discovery Bay ,Hong Kong
2011 HK Gold Coast (book signing exhibition)
2009 Solo Painting Exhibition The Avenue of Stars
Group Exhibition of Daniel Anderson workshop Classical Realism class of 2008 at Manhattan,NY
2007 Guest and Exhibition The Peak Galleria Hong Kong
2007 Invited workshop exhibition, Elements, Hong Kong
Group Exhibition of Classical Realism class of 2007 at Manhattan,NY
2006 Collection by Cardinal Zen Ze-kiun and exhibited at Catholic Church of Hong Kong.
2004 - 2007, Hong Kong Young Artist Group Exhibition, Hong Kong Central Library.
Group Exhibition of Classical Realism class of 2006 at East Village, Manhattan,NY
2005 Illustration original exhibition for Kung Kao Po
2004 Group Exhibition, Wanchai Tower
2003 Group Exhibition, Hong Kong Convention and Exhibition Centre,
2003 Winner of I luv Hong Kong Painting Competition, exhibition at The Landmark (Hong Kong).
2002 The Holy story Picture Book illustrated picture original exhibition ,sai wan ho civic centre.

SELECTED COLLECTIONS :

Cardinal of the Catholic Church Joseph Zen Ze-kiun
Organic Beauty Inc
Agriculture, Fisheries and Conservation Department
Ms.Ho Wei Ying
Ms. Annie Yu
Daniel Anderson
MR.Tsang Yan Sam

PUBLICATIONS :

Fisheye magazine , featured artist interview , November 2002
Kung Kao Po , interview , June 2006
Art of Rock Realism , 2008
The Art of Michael Andrew Law , 2010
December to Remember One man Show Art Book , 2013
iEgoism , 2015

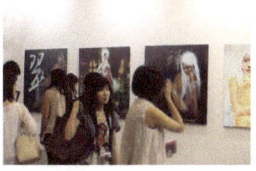

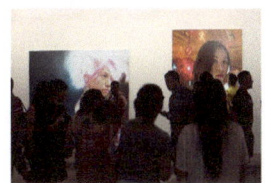

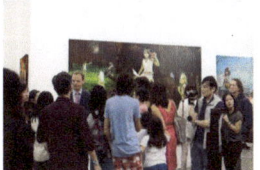

Solo Shows 2010 - 2013

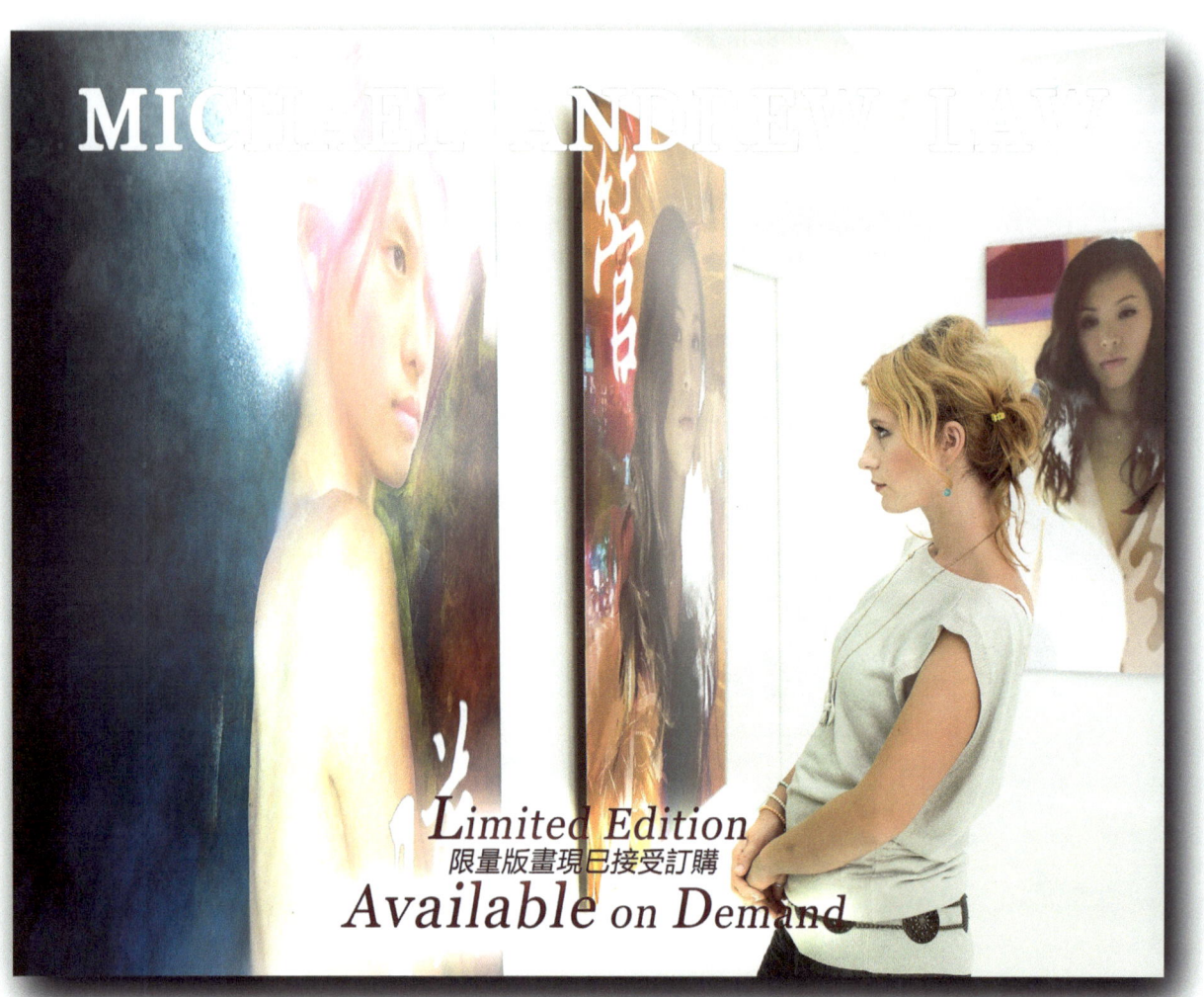

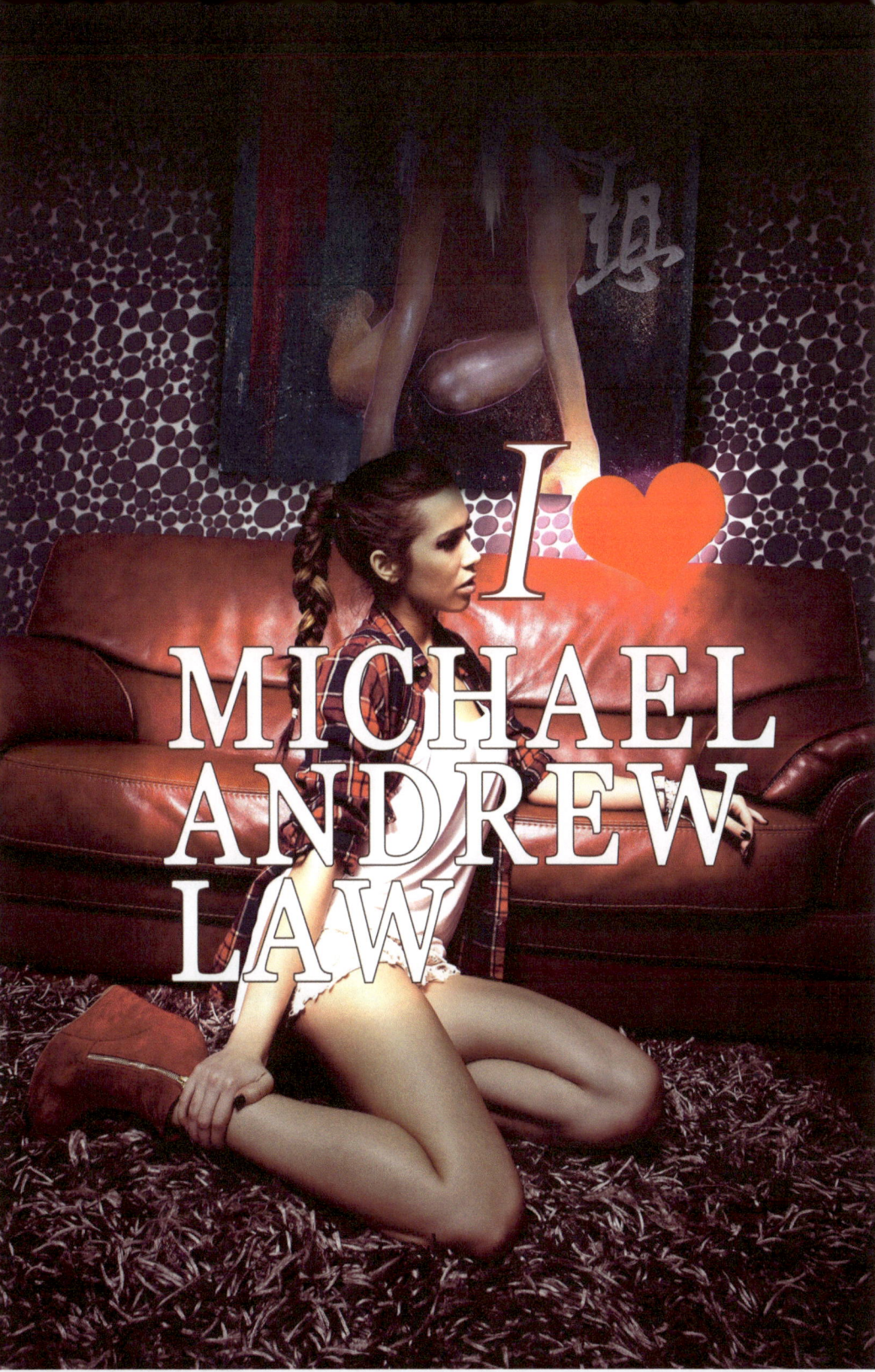

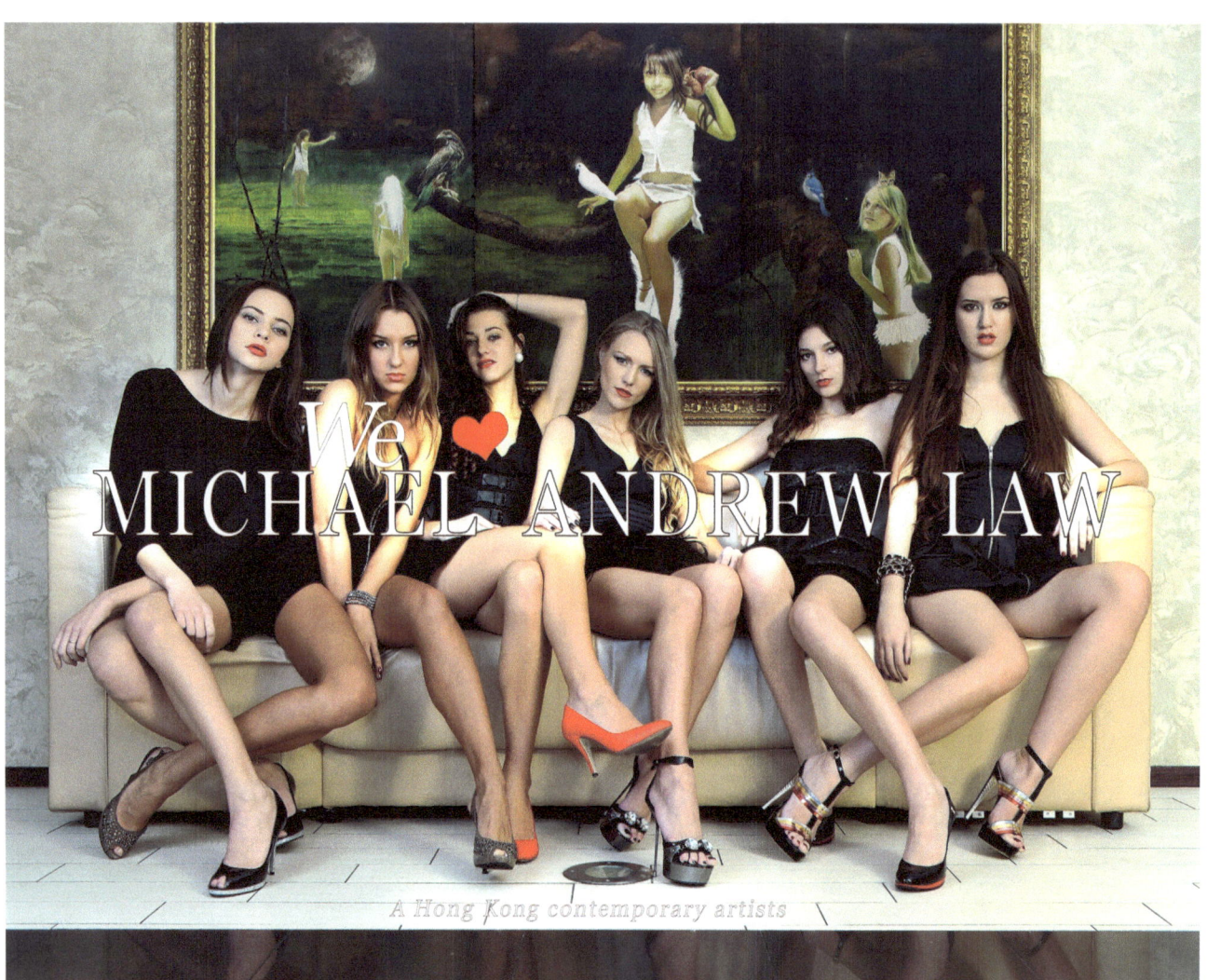

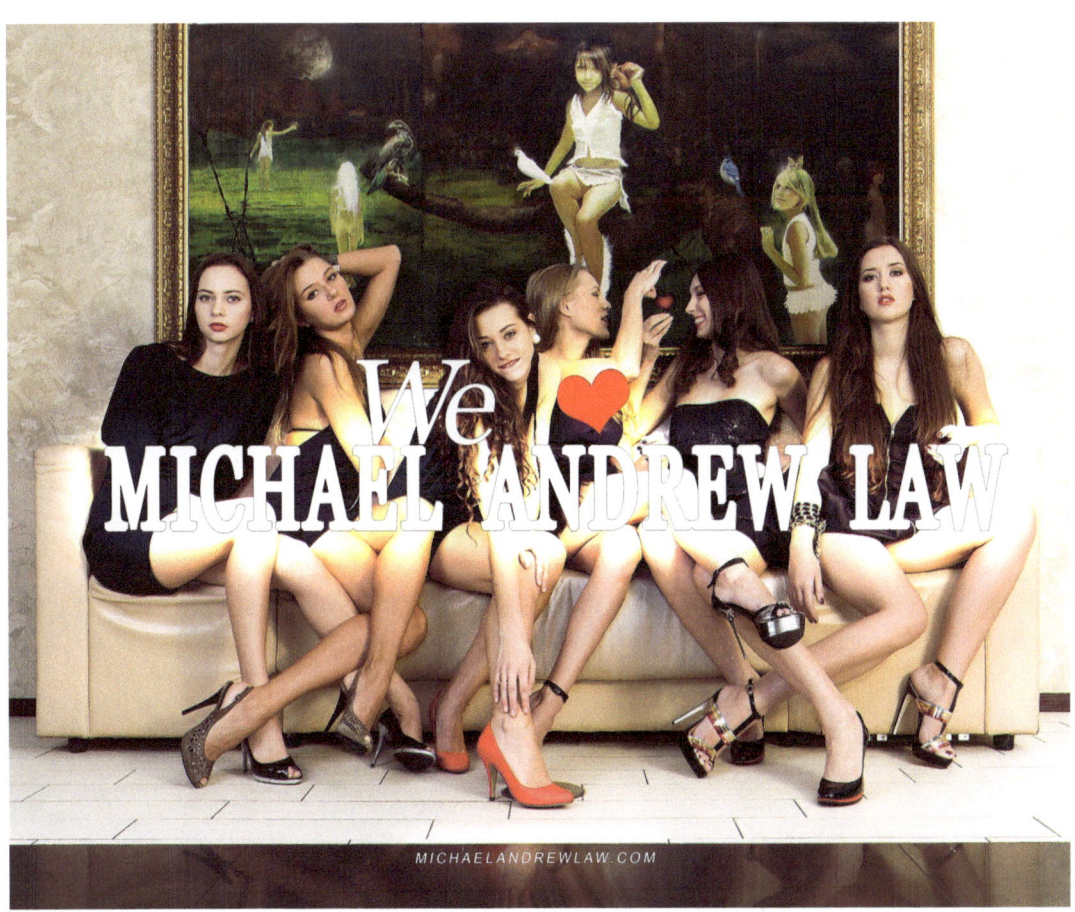

We ♥ MICHAEL ANDREW LAW

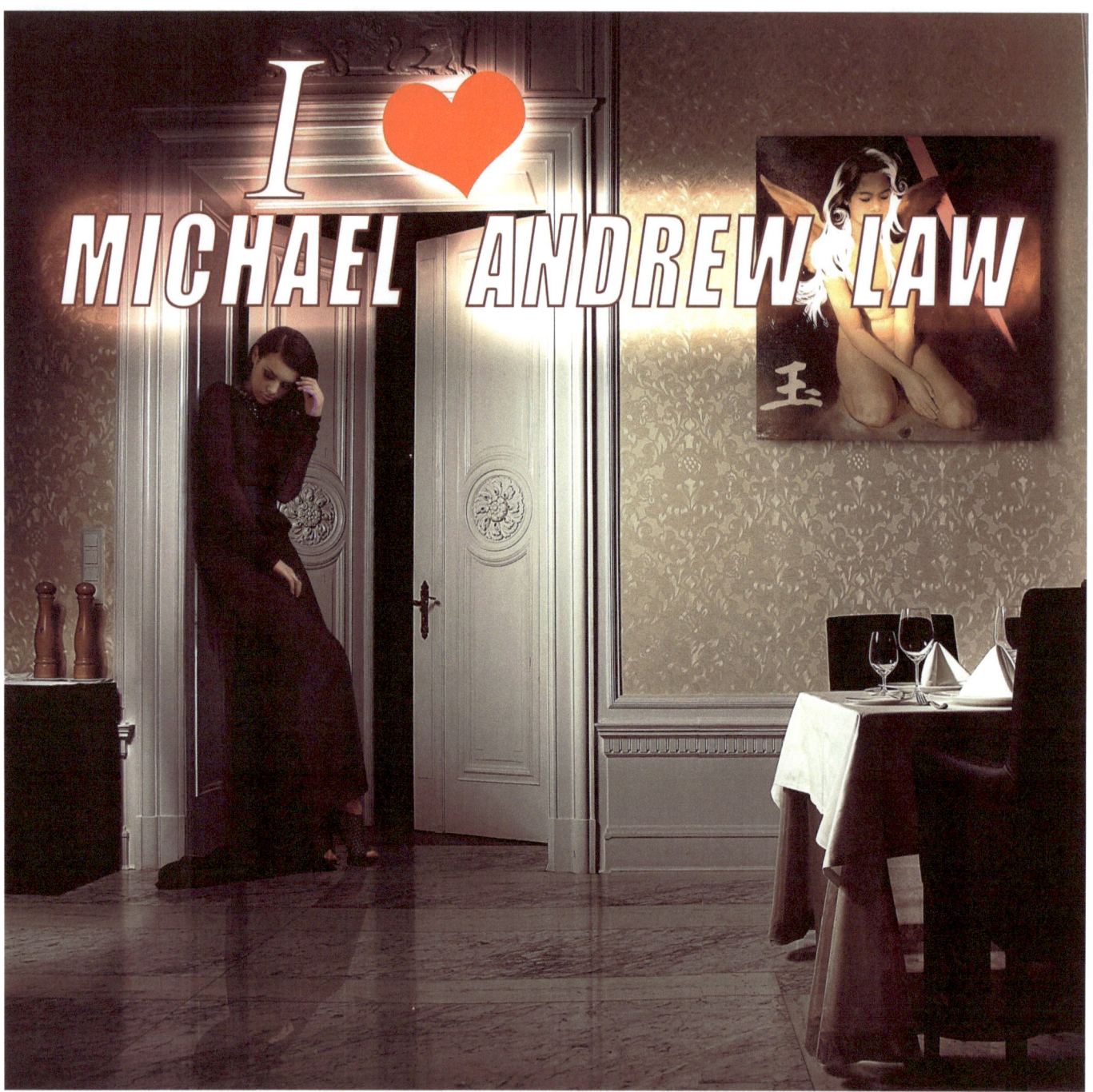

www.ingramcontent.com/pod-product-compliance
Lightning Source LLC
Chambersburg PA
CBHW040747200526
45159CB00023B/1766